Th

Of

Stoicism

JOHN TURNER

Table of Contents

Introduction

Thanks for choosing this book about Stoicism, I'd really love to hear your opinion, so make sure to leave a short review on Amazon if you enjoy it. It means a lot to me!

Stoicism is not some new age trend. If anything, it is a way of life practiced by the Romans thousands of years ago. It was a guide to life back then. But how about our world, the 21st-century one we are living in right now? Can Stoicism be used today? From the 80s up until today, modern day philosophers have all been interested in the works of the founding fathers of Stoicism- Seneca, Nero, Epictetus as well as Marcus Aurelius and the objective is to draw on their ideas and repackage them as guidance to live life in today's environment.

Philosophers of Stoicism today, such as William Irvine, Ryan Holiday and Massimo Pigliucci all, write about the benefits of following the Stoic way of life with the conviction that Stoicism practiced daily is the key to a happy and good life which focuses on our mental state and the virtues of being rational. It explores the Ideal life, a life that is in sync with nature and practicing a calm indifference towards events that are out of our control.

Stoicism is a line of philosophy that involves personal ethics and is indoctrinated along with the principle of logic and its views on the natural world. The school of stoicism was founded in 300 BC Greece by Zeno of Citium and is heavily influenced by the teachings of Socrates.

1

During this time in Greece, Stoicism was immensely popular and flourished for several hundreds of years as a way to live by the different people of diverse backgrounds in Greece. Because of its philosophy, stoics were considered to be cold, passive and stone like figures.

Despite the phrase 'to remain stoic' or to remain indifferent, the Stoics were anything but indifferent to the reality of life. In truth, they were active participants of the world and they used this philosophy to reason and reach out to others in a state of everlasting joy, tranquility, mental fortitude, and character excellence.

In this book, we will explore the reality of Stoicism, its history and most importantly, the principles of Stoicism.

This book will also attempt to help you use Stoicism in everything you do and weave in Stoic exercises and principles into your daily life.

You will also go through the Stoic view of optimism as well as emotions.

You do not have to baptize yourself a Stoic to practice these values and principles. When you continue reading this book, you will come to understand why. The Greek Stoic philosopher Epictetus put it this way: *"There is only one way to happiness and that is to cease worrying about things which are beyond the power of our will."*

Let's journey into a life philosophy that will help you look at the world a different way. Stoic or not, this philosophy can be practiced at any point in our lives.

Chapter 1

Stoicism Defined

To give stoicism a definition to better understand it, stoicism can be defined as a way life that teachers a person methods and ways to maintain a rational, calm state of mind no matter what events unfold in front of us.

Stoicism helps us focus on the things that we all can control- our own reaction and actions towards a certain scenario or event. Through this mentality, we can then focus on issues that we can control and not be so worried about the things that we cannot. This is probably why the term 'to remain stoic' was created, which is to remain indifferent no matter what is happening around us. Of course, this definition covers just the tip of the iceberg of what Stoicism is about.

History of Stoicism

Founded in 301 BC, Stoicism has come a long way in its train of thought, infusing thoughts and principles that relate with the modern world. First preachers by Zeno of Citium, a Phoenician merchant Stoicism was first known as Zenonism but eventually became to be known as Stoicism, a change in name based on the location that the followers used to originally meet, which was at Stoa Poikile, also referred to as the Painted Porch.

Followers of this school of philosophy often met in public places where anyone could join the conversation, listen to the preaching and debates. At some point, stoicism was also known as a 'philosophy of the street,' and it was usually ordinary folk who were amongst its biggest followers, together with a small number of aristocrats.

From the get-go and for the next five centuries after that, Stoicism has remained among the most popular and influential schools of philosophy. It is also known as a famous civic discipline in the West and was practiced by all walks of life, all different layers of the community, whether rich or poor. Everyone was in the pursuit of the Good Life.

At some point, Stoicism went under the radar and with it, the core knowledge and principles faded and were almost forgotten until the 1970s when Stoicism was revived again. Stoicism came into the spotlight again because of Cognitive Behavioral Therapy (CBT). Authors like Ryan Holiday and William Irvine used Stoicism philosophical inspiration to write about the need for it in our society today.

Leaders of Stoicism

- Marcus Aurelius

Famously referred to as the last good emperor, Marcus Aurelius was also the most powerful man on earth at that time. He reflected every evening on the day's ongoings and wrote down his thoughts and observations in his diary, which would go on to be published as 'Meditations.' It would become one of the most important, profound and significant sources of Stoic Philosophy.

- Epictetus

Born a slave but become a legend, that is the life of Epictetus. Epictetus was also the teacher to other great minds of ancient Rome such as Marcus Aurelius and founded his own school. His teachers have been meticulously recorded by his student, Arrian in the book called Discourses and Enchiridion. Enchiridion, meaning 'ready at hand' is often translated as a handbook and meant to be used like a sword ready to be drawn at the slightest sign of danger or threat. The handbook was a way to deal with life's challenges.

- Seneca

Seneca was known as many things from Rome's best playwright to the wisest broker to Nero's tutor and adviser, Seneca's personal letters survived and served as some of the most sought-after sources of Stoic philosophy. These manuscripts survived despite being forced to commit suicide by Nero. The documents from these leaders of stoicism form the foundations of Stoicism.

Principles of Stoicism

To understand stoicism is to know its principles.

#1 Living in agreement with Nature

Eudaimonia was the central theme for all ancient schools of philosophy and it was the ultimate goal of life. This ultimate goal of life was the supreme happiness attainable by human beings.

The Good Life that the Stoics refer to summed up the idea as 'living in agreement with nature.' This was the goal and the central slogan of Stoicism.

Living in agreement with nature is about behaving rationally as a human being. We must always aim to live our virtues and apply human reasoning to all our actions. Only when we do this, we truly live in agreement with nature, the way humans are meant to behave.

#2 Living by Virtue

Achieving virtue is the highest good that one can attain as a stoic. There are four cardinal virtues in Stoicism:

- Wisdom or prudence
- Justice or fairness
- Courage or fortitude
- Self-discipline or temperance

Here the term virtue lies in excelling at your own character's strength and applying reason that is in a manner that is both praiseworthy as well as healthy.

Acting according to virtue more often than not, brings about benefits. These benefits, however, should be seen as an added bonus rather than the primary motive for your actions. This is why reasoning comes into play. You always apply reason in order to do the right thing and act according to wisdom, courage, justice, and self-discipline.

On another note, the results of your virtuous actions may not always be positive ones. Which is why you shouldn't make it your main motive. By focusing on what you can control (your actions), you are already practicing virtue.

#3 Only Focus on the things Within your Control

A major part of stoicism is the ability to distinguish what elements and issues or scenarios that we can control or within our power and what elements or situations that are beyond our control or out of our power.

Things that are 'up to us' are usually voluntary choices related to our actions as well as our judgments. Everything else beyond that is not under our control.

For example, if you are trying to lose weight; that is what you can control are your diet and fitness. But you do not have control over the genes that you were born into or other factors such as hormonal imbalance, injuries or illnesses.

The idea here is that we are all responsible for our own growth and because all that matters in life are up to us. The takeaway here is to focus on our efforts and attention to the elements that we have greater power over- leave the rest of the universe.

#4 Understanding the Difference between Indifferent, Bad and Good

In Stoicism, things that are bad, that are good, and indifferent have a stark and extremely vivid difference. Stoics refer to good things such as wisdom, justice, courage, and self-discipline, which are all Stoic virtues. The bad things are those opposite of these virtues, which are cowardice, injustice, folly, and indulgence.

When it comes to indifferent things, it is usually life and death, bad reputation and fame, pleasure as well as pain, poverty and wealthy as well as health and sickness. Stoic indifferent things are the kinds of things the modern society would judge as bad or good. However, in Stoicism, these indifferent things do not play a major role in the quest for the Good Life.

Essentially, indifferent things do no matter whether you are rich or poor, sick or healthy. It does not play a huge role in ultimate happiness. We need to be satisfied with whatever nature gives us and be indifferent towards indifferent things.

#5 Taking Action

You are the master of your own ship and in order to attain the Good Life, you cannot just lay back and expect things to happen as is. To live the Stoic way of life or in other words, the eudaimonic life, you would need to always endeavor to do the right thing. Stoics are known to be doers, but it is not enough only to think about your own life. As a Stoic, you need to take action and do things differently. Stoics must earn a good life by taking the necessary and right actions.

Learning how to live your life should also involve applying these ideas.

#6 Asking What Could Go Wrong?

As humans, we are more prone to think about what could go wrong as opposed to what could go right. So this principle of 'What could go wrong' actually sits nicely among modern society. Stoic thinking is to always prepare oneself for future events in order to stay calm in the face of adversity.

Take for example if you are planning an event and you have done all that the necessary things that you needed to from managing the guest list, to finalizing the caterer, the itinerary, decorations are up. Now, you stand back and ask yourself 'What could go wrong?', or 'What could happen that doesn't go as planned?''.

Figuring out what would happen outside the plan can help you prepare a backup plan.

7 Accepting the Outcome of Things Beyond Control

In Stoicism, we are all meant to do the right thing and try our best to get there, but in the same time, we are also meant to accept the outcome of things beyond our control. While we need to give it our all, we also must accept that there are outcomes that are beyond our direct control. This is the key to confidence and trusting in your own self.

- To do your extreme best
- Understand that results are beyond your control
- To accept whatever that has happened
- To continue to live and act virtuously

#8 Amor Fati – Love Everything that Happens

Another good principle in Stoicism is called the "art of acquiescence" – to accept rather than fight every little thing.

In most events or scenarios that have taken place especially those that have gone south, we can only change our opinions on them and not the event itself, unless we had a time machine and could go back in time. So, we can only accept what has happened and look forward to these two steps:

To accept that we don't control everything that happens. We

simply must accept it.

To not only accept, but even love everything that happens. We simply get to enjoy it. It is hard to feel grateful or happy for something that we never wanted to take place, but things happen for a reason and whether it is the desired effect or an unexpected outcome, it happened specifically for you.

You may not understand why it happened, but eventually, you will and you will see how it benefited you.

#9 Turning Problems into Opportunities

Perception is what shapes our outlook on life, how we see the world around us, how we engage with it and how we interpret the things that happen to us. By now, you already know that in Stoicism, events beyond our control are not seen as good or bad but indifferent.

And our perception towards these events boils down to how we choose to look at them and respond to them- it is all that matters. You may choose to look at yourself as a failure when things don't go according to your way and you do not attempt to not take on that challenge again OR you could learn from these failures and choose to take on the challenge again and improve it for round two.

We are not affected by the actual events but by our judgment of these events.

In Stoicism, you need to:

1. to look at the events objectively
2. choose to use them for their best

How you see these events is so much more important because you can find the good in everything. In Stoicism, it is all about looking at things as an opportunity for growth.

#10 Practising Mindfulness

At the end of the day, you need to be mindful of everything that you do. To live according to the Stoic philosophy, you need to be mindful of the actions you because ultimately, all stoic principles are about being more mindful. This also means that you need to be your very own check and balance- monitoring and observing your own thoughts and actions towards situations. You must also be more mindful and aware of each step you take in life. When you practice Stoicism, you need to know when to take a step by from your thoughts and also decide on your best action towards certain scenarios.

Chapter 2

The Benefits of Stoicism

The ultimate life goal for Stoics is to live purposefully and carefully. When we are honest with the way we live, it's anything but difficult to perceive how simple (and normal) it is to spend life by accident.

In Stoicism, the principles we learned in the first chapter can be summarized as:

- To be clear about what your intentions are in everything that you do
- To be thoughtful about your choices
- To be simple in your desires and
- To be content with what you can control

What are the benefits of leading a life based on Stoic principles? Essentially, each individual benefits differently based on what they are going through at the moment in life, but to give you an idea of what you can expect in this modern day, here are the benefits associated with Stoicism:

#1 You learn to articulate life with a deeper sense of meaning

How much do you align yourself with your purpose each day? Some of us go about life by taking care of other pressing concerns that are not related to us and eventually, these pressing concerns become our lives. In this time, we have forgotten who we are and what our visions are. What kind of life do you want? What kind of parent do you want to be- the ever-present one or the compassionate one? What about the kind of partner you deem yourself to be- the committed? The activist?

What do you want people to remember you as? What kind of legacy do you want to leave behind?

It isn't wrong to be the things described above because all of these things contribute to a positive outcome. A compassionate parent produces a well-adjusted child. A devoted partner enables their partner to achieve success; a goal-oriented entrepreneur enriches a community.

Essentially, some people will be happy with what they have while others are happy with who they are. Stoicism enables us to appreciate these differences. Better guidance is not about asking what we want but more of the kind of person we want to become. This is your mantra each day.

#2 You become more grateful

Stoicism pushes for virtues and when we live by virtues, we tend to look at the circumstances of our actions. While not all our actions are positive ones, the stoicism belief is to be grateful because life is a balance of positives and negatives.

When we focus on the indifferent things, we do not attach ourselves to the positives or the negatives but recognize the balance of living in agreement with nature.

We all have trouble seeing the gratitude in scenarios and events we encounter each day and it is only because we are not seeing much of what we encounter. It is about looking at ourselves and understanding how fortunate we are to be alive and it is also about looking back in our day today and see what we've accomplished, no matter how little the task, like for example- completing this book. Look back and see what events worked in your favor and also what you learned and how you reacted when things didn't work in your favor.

We all receive either something good or something affirming each day- it depends on how we perceive things.

#3 You learn to live with boundaries

When discussing boundaries here, we are not talking about walls or enclosures we lock ourselves in- whether emotionally, physically, mentally or spiritually. It is not about isolating ourselves or living outside the community. It is about acknowledging what resources we have and how to work with it and these resources are limited time and limited energy.

Let's face- we always face limited time and also limited energy; otherwise, we would be running and doing things all day, every day. Living within our boundaries enables us to manage our time and energy efficiently and this means paying attention to the things that matter the most instead of giving into negativity such as anger, resentment, and worry.

Not giving in to these unhelpful emotions enable us to focus on our vision and the people that matter most in our lives.

Consider looking at your relationships that foster well-being and serve to contribute to the vision in your life. Invest your time and energy in these things that sustain your equanimity and let the rest go.

There is absolutely nothing wrong with being selective of where to invest your time and energy. At the end of the day, it makes you a more useful person not only to your goals and vision but to the community you live in and the people you connect to.

#4 Learn to live with not getting what you want (i.e., create a detachment practice)

This principle helps us to let go of attachment in life and again, living in agreement with nature. It is also to be mindful and be able to understand is still great despite not getting what we want on our wish list.

Life presents itself with enough challenges and we do not need to set ourselves up with even more challenges by fueling it with expectations. Here, the principle of perception is practiced. The thing is, there is absolutely nothing in this life of ours is guaranteed, except death. But this is nothing new- we all know this and there's no point getting depressed about it. We need to embrace it and this should be a driving force to focus and invest in relationships that are meaningful and worth your time, one that we enjoy and hold on to these positive relationships till the end or at least as long as we can.

#5 We learn to apply a control grid

If you feel that there are too many things clouding over you and preventing you from thinking straight or dealing with all sorts of issues, then here is a good time to breathe and get out your graph paper.

Think about principle Amor Fati, Love Everything that Happens, and start listing the things you have complete control over and then the things you have some form of control over and finally, the ones that you absolutely have no control over. Be as honest as you can. There are times that these things may be about family, work and your finances that you may or may not have control over.

What is the benefit of doing this? Well, for one, you will be more efficient in applying your efforts as well as your time and energy into what you can control.

You will also be able to accept the things that you cannot control and love the things that are happening and enjoy it as it happens.

#6 You learn to accept your life as "on loan."

Stoicism applied well into our modern lives enables us to lead a more simplistic and happy life.

It is always good to take a step back once in a while and look at all that you have done in your life and realize that your life… is all on a loan.

Not to get morbid or anything, but essentially, when you realize that all your work, money, kids, partners, friends, parents, land, talents, possessions, as well as joy and grief, is just temporary, you will truly feel more gratitude and you will be able to enjoy you while it lasts.

Life will continue to go on even when you no longest cease to exist. And this is a good thing- you want people you care and love to continue living without grief or pain. You can file it under religion or you can file it under the metaphysical or you can file this under nature or the laws of evolutions or the meaning of life- whatever you want.

Knowing that life is temporary makes it easier to look at things from a different perspective.

Bottom Line

Stoicism wants us to live life more lightly, more purposefully and more deliberately. It is not about just us and it is not meant to detach ourselves from everything else that is happening around us. When we become more aware of the things that we can control and realize the amount of effort we want to put into our relationships, we become more mindful of our time and our energy as well as our thoughts. We are more tuned in to what life brings us and are happier with our lives.

Chapter 3

Understanding the Stoic Sense of Emotions

When you continue reading this book, you would find that the overriding theme is how Stoics view disasters or problems as possible opportunities. Sometime even when faced with the death of a dear one, a Stoic will always fall back to the reasoning of 'there is good behind this,' or they would have already thought about the worst case scenario before it happens, in order for them to look at the current situation with a more rational mind.

But, we're humans and we come with a range of emotions. Wouldn't crying over the love of a friend or family help us in the grieving process? Don't Stoics cry?

In this chapter, we will look into the whole sense of emotions from the Stoic perspective. This chapter is extremely important because only then will you truly understand why Stoics think the way they do. Only then will you grasp the idea of emotions from the Stoical perspective.

In stoicism, there are three 'Good Feelings' that are recognized, which are called *hai eupatheiai* in Greek. These three good emotions are:

- Joy vs. Pleasure
- Wish vs. Appetite

- Caution vs. Fear

These good emotions are contrasted with the three Passions or 'Bad Feelings' in the Stoic philosophy, as explained above.

For many people getting immersed in the philosophy of Stoicism, the main issue that is always brought up is that Stoicism does not allow room for emotions or passions to develop. It promotes the idea that suppresses emotions and advocates an unemotional, apathetic and passionless life.

It is not about Rejecting Emotions, rather its rejecting passions.

Stoics view on emotions are not the same as how the rest of society views it or defines it. In today's world, the word 'emotions' usually refers to a mental feeling that is often contrasted with reason.

When you understand emotion in this sense, then, according to Sellars, "the Stoics do not reject emotions, they reject passions, and that is quite a different thing."

The Stoics also believed that as human beings, we should:

- Cultivate concern and care as well as the empathy towards family and friends
- Acknowledge that external events will affect us in some way
- That we will have natural reactions towards events such as being shocked or scared

For example, if you heard an explosion, you would probably jump behind a wall- this is not passion.

On another note, if you hear that you may be losing your job, then you're bound to be feeling fearful and anxious- this is passion.

At times like these, the Stoic principle is to eliminate negative reactions by thinking about the why. So for instance, say if we lose our jobs, it may not be as bad as we think things would get. It may be a little difficult but not entirely bad the way we think of it in our heads. Ultimately, the Stoics believed that our reactions are usually a result of poor perceptions and poor thinking.

The Stoic's List of Good Passions

The Stoics believe that the only good kind of passions is the ones that are virtues which puts the mind in a healthy state. This is considered the only truthful good and the one thing that can guarantee happiness. Good passions often follow mental climates that produce proper and good reasoning.

As John Stellar quotes it:

"The ideal Stoic life is thus far from unemotional in the English sense of the word"

In this principle, the Stoics reject the faulty reasoning that is a result of judgments that are confused with positive values and all the negative consequences that comes with it.

What is Passion to the Stoic?

To summarize a little bit, so we are all on the same understanding, our modern sense of emotions is not the same as what the Stoics refer to.

The word emotion is Passion in Stoicism, but since we are all more comfortable using the modern word emotion, for this next discussion, we will continue referring to Passion = Emotion.

To make it easier, we will go with EorP.

The first definition relates to EorP being an impulse or force. These things happen to anyone and are often contrasted with the things we do or the actions we take.

For example, EorP is like running downhill but not being able to stop. Instead, the force propels you forward. EorP also has a temporal dimension which is usually strong at present and over time, it starts to weaken. On the 2nd or 3rd definitions, it emphasizes greatly on disrupt reasons.

Often, EoPr misrepresents an item's value and this then misleads our impulses towards wanting to achieve it. For instance, let's look at wealth. Pursuing it without being mindful only leads to a life lived poorly as we lack all the goodness that comes with life.

On another instance, say if we want to take revenge on someone and we act on it based on an angry impulse, this means that it could lead us to commit a crime (since we did not think about this rationally in the first place) and the consequence would be dealing with the law and ending up in jail.

EorP is based on bad reasoning.

The last definition of EorP is as "a fluttering in the soul." This definition is derived from the Stoic's sense that EorP has a physical basis, which leads to a physical consequence. It is like a relationship between heart rate and blood pressure

In most Stoic teachings, you will often find that the primary Passions that the Stoics identify with are related to appetite and fear. The general idea is, if we think of something is good and pure, we tend to pursue it, but when we think of something being not good or bad, we end up fearing it.

These Passions, according to the Stoics, are often related to either Distress or Pleasure. When we satisfy our appetites, we experience pleasure, but when we fail to satisfy them, we end up getting distressed over it. If we end up fearing something, we also end up feeling distressed, but when this fear does not manifest or happen the way we imagine it to be, then we experience pleasure.

Is having too much of emotions bad for us?

Any kind of excessive emotion, if you think about it- is bad. Anything excessive is bad and you probably didn't need the Stoics to tell you that. Experiencing EorP excessively can cause errors in judgment whether it is between the bad and the good, the past, the present or the future.

At first, it may seem pleasurable, but eventually, it will become bad for us. Excessive EorP brings about bad judgments. If our satisfaction for appetites for things like food and drink, material possessions or even sex brings us less pleasure than we anticipated, this could mean that you have indulged into it too much.

The Stoics believed that it isn't worth the risk for more important things such as health in the pursuit of bad passions. In another way, the things that we fear, such as pain, anxiety, and humiliation may not be as bad as we thought. We cannot stop living just because we are paralyzed with fear.

The Role of Emotions

The Stoics never rejected Passions but strive towards living a balanced emotional life. If you think of pleasure, the Stoics think of it as joy. If you think of it as fear, the Stoics think of it as caution. If you feel there's appetite, the Stoics look at it as reasonable hope. As for distress, the Stoics reject it completely.

You should act as a result of rational deliberation. For example, you may want to lead a healthier lifestyle but do not attempt to run every day or take heavyweights- this is considered excessive. If you are considering living by the principles of Stoicism, then it is may be hard at first to draw the line between excessive and restrained EorP. But clearly, as you practice a balance, you will live a better life when reason prevents us from becoming slaves to our passions and desires.

Calmness in the Face of Adversity

Sometimes, whether we like it or not, we get sucked into other people's drama or get involved in office politics or we are affected by the issues that are happening in our community.

Most of the time, we did not ask to be involved or to be sucked in or to be affected. Things just happen. Negativity spreads like cancer and as much as you do not like it, you end up having to deal with it or having to deal with the consequences of it.

Imagine a life where the things that trouble everyone else did not trouble you?

What if you lived a life when everyone else got mad or upset or greedy but you like a champion, remained calm, clear-headed and objective?

Well, in truth, you can actually be this way. That is what Stoicism strives to educate its followers on. The Stoic ideas seek to give you plenty of power, the coolness of a cucumber and the serenity of a calm mind.

Your top priority goal is to build an inner fortress that enables you to stay calm and even untouchable when you are faced with adversity. You do not need to give into events excessive attention than what it already has. We do not want to be slaves to our own impulses and be pushed around by external events.

This is not something that is easy to do but with some practice, effort, and know-how, we can get closer to this unflappable calmness.

#1 Concern yourself with only your actions

"Happiness and freedom begin with a clear understanding of one principle: Some things are within our control, and some things are not. It is only after you have faced up to this fundamental rule and learned to distinguish between what you can and can't control that inner tranquility and outer effectiveness become possible."
— Epictetus

All of us can be so many good things from good to kind, patient to forgiving. But no matter what we do, we cannot control the outcome of these actions. Life has a wicked sense of humor. You may think you're doing all the right things, but then your partner will leave you. You may think you're being the best team player in your department only to be let go by management. You may think that you're eating the best and healthier food, but you'd end up with cancer. Rather than worrying yourself about that what ifs and what mays which you cannot control, you can just look inside you and control only your character, your actions, and your reactions.

How you act and treat people may not necessarily influence the way they will treat you. You may be kind and helpful, but this does not mean all of them will appreciate your kindness and goodness. Your patience will be tested and even your love towards your partner questioned. These are outcomes you have no control of and in no way would be able to influence. You also have no control over what people think of you. Some may react in the way you envision, but some may think otherwise of you. You can influence them, but you cannot control their actions or thoughts or opinions about you. The only thoughts and opinions you can control are that of your own.

#2 Do good without thinking if it will be noticed

"An emerald shines even if its worth is not spoken of."
– Marcus Aurelius

If you want to do well, do well but don't look and see if others can see the goodness you are doing. Do good because they are good and not because you want to be liked or loved or even respected.

When it comes to doing good in the Stoic book, you'd be surprised that it mirrors the kind of teachings we've all heard of before. When it comes to doing good work, for the Stoic, it's all about doing good hard work because hard work is good and not because it will bring you good things.

When it comes to love, love because giving your love to someone is a good thing, not because you also want to be loved back.

When it comes to being fair to others, do it because it is the right thing to do and not because you expect to be treated the same way should the time come.

You want to do something because the reward is just that it is good and not because you want something out of it. Only you can control your goodness so your efforts and energy should be focused on you.

#3 Do not blindly accept or reject criticism

"If someone is able to show me that what I think or do is not right, I will happily change, for I seek the truth, by which no one was ever truly harmed. It is the person who continues in his self-deception and ignorance who is harmed."
– Marcus Aurelius

Evaluate the criticism you receive and change for the better. You were not made perfect and acknowledging this is the first step to self-improvement. We are able to lead a calmer more serene life if we know that deep down, we have made the best effort to become a better version of ourselves.

As long as we are putting in an honest effort to improve, our conscience will be clear. Do not dig a hole of self-deception because this is ultimately a trap that we create for ourselves. It tears down and claws us down when we least expect it. This leads us into a dark abyss of certainty, where we do not know what troubles us.

#4 Do not fear the unknown

"Wild animals run from the dangers they actually see, and once they have escaped them worry no more. We, however, are tormented alike by what is past and what is to come. A number of our blessings do us harm, for memory brings back the agony of fear while foresight brings it on prematurely. No one confines his unhappiness to the present." – Seneca

The Stoics believe that people are born with only two fears, which are the fear of falling and the fear of loud noises. The rest of our fears originate from our past and these fears become a reality in our future. We are rarely ever afraid of the things in our present. We may fear loneliness not because we are alone today, but we fear that we may be forever alone.

#5- Train to focus your thoughts and goals

"To be everywhere is to be nowhere." – Seneca

Low attention spans, wanderlust, fear of commitment are all the human desire to be everywhere or risk the fear of missing out.

With the internet, we are more unfocused than we were before because it enables us to be everywhere at once and yet at the same time, nowhere. The more and more we are hounded by mobile phones and laptops, smartphones and other gadgets, we lose our ability and desire to focus.

It isn't to say that you MUST always focus on one thing or only be one certain place all the time or hang out with just one person. The mind also needs relaxation to explore your own thoughts.

Thinking about too many things and too many issues can be detrimental. Having an aimless mind with your location always changing and your options always open, you will run into purposelessness. You will end up being everywhere but nowhere and this does not make for an interesting person nor a calm person. You will find out that not one thing or one place can ever satisfy you.

#6 Control your mind and your attitude

"If you really want to escape the things that harass you, what you're needing is not to be in a different place but to be a different person." – Seneca

People are often led to believe that the reason for their unhappiness is because of the circumstance that they are in. They are always led to believe that if only they had one chance at a pleasant situation, they would be much happier.

However, as mentioned before, you will never be able to control a situation you are in full.

Life at any given moment can take a turn for the worst and while this is something that you cannot control, you can, however, control your mind and attitude towards this scenario. Never let anything or anyone harass you without your permission- you can deny this at any given moment.

Practice Misfortune
(Ask What Could Go Wrong)

As humans, we are more prone to think about what could go wrong as opposed to what could go right. So this principle of 'What could go wrong' actually sits nicely among modern society.

Stoic thinking is to always prepare oneself for future events in order to stay calm in the face of adversity.

According to William Irvine, author of the book A Guide to the Good Life, described it as "the single most valuable technique in the Stoics' toolkit" and termed it 'negative visualization.' the only difference is that these scenarios of what could go wrong are not negative ones, but they are 'indifferent'.

Take for example if you are planning an event and you have done all that the necessary things that you needed to from managing the guest list to finalizing the caterer, the itinerary, decorations are up. Now, you stand back and ask yourself 'What could go wrong?, or 'What could happen that doesn't go as planned?''.

Figuring out what would happen outside the plan can help you prepare a backup plan.

Negative Visualization as a Powerful Tool

Negative visualization deals with one of the most important issues in Stoicism, which is to prepare for anything and everything that may come your way.

It is sort of like foresight. Before something could happen, Stoics look at the possibilities of what could go wrong or what obstacle may crop up or what difficulties could happen.

In using negative visualization, there are three elements we can look at, which are:

1. What's the key idea?
2. Why it wasn't actually 'negative' to the Stoics.
3. Why so pessimistic?

What's the Key Idea of the Stoic Exercise 'Negative Visualization'?

The idea is clear and simple. All you need to do is to visualize the possibility of something going wrong. Basically, you are putting out all the scenarios that could go wrong so that if they occur, you will stay calm and cool. Staying calm and cool enables you to respond in the best way possible.

A stoic's main goal is to attain the Good Life and to reach is that to live in accordance with virtues from courage to wisdom, justice, and temperance. In order to live according to these virtues, Stoics mentally train themselves.

In all honesty, it is easy to live according to virtues when life goes on as planned. But would you still be able to when things don't go on as planned, such as when you encounter illness or death or exile?

By regularly visualizing misfortunes, Stoics prepare for the worst and live in a virtuous manner when they have occurred and they referred to this exercise as premeditation Malorum to train themselves to stay calm and free despite the emotional suffering that they face or when bad situations have happened.

Modern Stoic philosopher, William Irvine was the one who coined the term 'negative visualization,' and by practicing to visualize negative scenarios, we decrease our fear for them and prepare ourselves to deal with the crises that occur. This kind of exercise is also used in Cognitive Behavioral Therapy (CBT).

Are the Misfortunes Imagined in Negative Visualization Really "Negative"?

Again, it is understandable if someone misconstrues the term negative visualization to mean something bad. It is misleading, no doubt.

But the thing is, the basic Stoic principle points out that external events can neither be positive nor negative but only indifferent, simply because they are out of our control.

The Stoics prefer focusing on what is within their control and not worrying about the things that are beyond their control. This is why the Stoics imagined as well as real 'misfortunes' are just not only negative ones but the ones that they do not have control over.

To put it in simple terms, the bad things that we imagine aren't really actually bad, but it has got to do with our response and reaction to it.

How to Practice Negative Visualization Step by Step

Before we move ahead on how to practice negative visualization, a quick reminder that negative visualization isn't just about preparing yourself to face the worst possible scenarios but also facing events and situations that you have no control of.

For example, a bad or negative situation could be the loss of a spouse. You get married and you are well aware that one day, either one of you will die. As a Stoic, you visualize what could happen in the event of spousal death. Before anything could occur, you prepare for the worst but ensuring that you both have your wills written, determine who gets what, how your properties would be divided, what happens to your retirement fund and bank accounts, what happens to your children and possessions.

A situation that you have no control of would be something like the electricity going off on one of your events. You plan everything from the decor to the napkins, making sure the chef cooks the steak as requested by all your guests, you make sure every bulb in every chandelier is working, you get the grass cut, the marble floors gleamed and then the day of the event happens and then, it suddenly goes dark. What do you do?

As a Stoic, you keep calm and rationalize the situation at hand. You have your electrician on standby- get them to check the circuits. Have you a generator on standby to- turn it on to bring lights to the main areas of the event while the electrician works on the circuits. You also prepared candles- get them out and charm your guests to dine under the soft lights of candles for a romantic night.

This is what negative visualization prepares us for. We ask what could go wrong in advance so that before a launch of a product, a start of a road trip or a commute to a job interview- you have plan B in case something should happen.

So in order to practice negative visualization, let's pull out the scenario going on a road trip.

Instead of imaging a most likely to happen scenario, try instead to imagine the worst-case scenario and the things that could go wrong, even if it is unlikely it could happen (like the Avenger's Civil War happening in your neighborhood).

Think of these scenarios as if it is happening at the very moment and not in the future. (the Avengers are fighting right about now)

What do you do in a situation like this? You're already in your van and someplace in the middle of town trying to get out to the freeway. What is the best you can do? Well, you can focus on what YOU CAN DO instead of panicking. Maybe wait till traffic subsides? Or find an alternative route out.

You can use the steps above to help you visualize what to do in an upcoming situation that you are getting yourself into. You will feel better prepared, mentally and physically.

We have the ability to work up an active and wild imagination, so visualizing these scenarios would be fairly easy.

You can also practice negative visualization as a post-mortem to an event. For example, the case of your spouse dying and you are overwhelmed with grief and sadness. What do you do? You prepare for dealing with these emotions by telling yourself that it was good while it lasted, that you enjoyed the times you had with them. It may not help immediately, but it will help in getting you out of a depressed mental state.

Conclusion

Negative visualization can be used at any time and for any specific events that you feel may incur some problems happening if you do not prepare for it beforehand. We can also do it periodically with general situations and events.

Chapter 4

Reemergence of Stoicism in the 21st Century

S toic teachings during the Middle Ages were generally related to issues concerning social and political focus. It eventually evolved in the Renaissance era with much of its focus geared towards Roman and Greek relics, to give a substratum to the second happening to Stoic perspectives in rationale, epistemology, and mysticism. This is the same for the documentation of the more recognizable Stoic conventions in morals and legislative issues. When it comes to the development of Stoicism towards the 21st century, here are some notable philosophers you need to know about:

- Justus Lipsius

Philosopher, humanist and philologist, Lipsius was a 16th century Flemish that was one of the revivers of Stoic doctrines. His most famous work is the *De Constantia*. His teachings also influenced a great many people, one of whom was the Baron de Montesquieu and political theorist Charles-Louis.

- Guillaume du Vair

A 17th-century French Christian lawyer and philosopher who focused his research and understanding of the Stoic moral code of conduct and made this version popular at the time. Together with him was Pierre Charron, the French skeptic, and theologian.

- Francis Bacon

Popularly recognized as the advocate of Lipsius teachings, he also encouraged the Stoic teachings related to modern philosophies of science. In the later Middle Ages, Stoicism doctrines also influenced many prominent figures in the Reformation and Renaissance periods, especially in the continuing war against the Aristotelianism.

- Pietro Pomponazzi

This 16th-century philosopher defended anti-scholastic Aristotelianism against the rising Averroists. Pomponazzi had strong Aristotelian roots and through his understanding of Stoicism, he adopted and advocated the Stoic view of freedom of will and providence.

- Leonardo Bruni

Like Pomponazzi, Bruni also adopted and advocated Stoic views regarding reason, fate, and fate-will. Bruni is a 15th-century humanist.

During this period, between the 15th and 16th century, there were plenty of books written about the philosophy of public law with a special focus on human nature and Stoic principles.

These books, such as De Jure Belli's 'On the Law of War & Peace' as well as Utopia by Thomas More and Hugo Grotius all discuss social rights, the theory of natural law and the Good Life of Stoicism.

- Huldrych Zwingli

Sixteenth-century Swiss reformer was a great advocate of subjective conviction as the new element of Christianity, which was in line with Stoic perspectives. This was especially related to the unrestrained choice and in addition on the outright destiny of the great and terrible individual, and on moral determinism.

- Herbert of Cherbury

Also known as the father of Deism would go on to develop the ideation of religious peace and the reducing of opposing views on religion, which are common elements. This view was soon to gain popularity and become a main theme in the 17th century.

- Philipp Melanchthon

This philosopher was also a great advocate of humanism and antiquity. The main motivation for him was Aristotle in spite of the fact that Melanchthon likewise took a gander at the Stoic hypothesis of information which trusts that inborn standards and the regular light of reason, which instruct the considerable certainties of mystical and good request.

Eventually, Stoicism was made the basis of the natural-law theory which reasons that the state is of direct divine origin and the independence of the church

In the seventeenth century, the Cartesian unrest acquired other Stoic understandings, for example, that profound quality is a mix of dutifulness to the law of reason, which God has presented to people morals surmises an intelligence of nature since people must figure out how to keep their place on the planet, for at exactly that point may they act appropriately

This self-checking is the premise of morals and the shared trait of truth bespeaks the view that lone considerations and will have a place with people as the body is of the material world. These perspectives were created by René Descartes and he is regularly hailed as the father of present-day reasoning, in his dualism of brain (or soul) and body.

- Benedict de Spinoza

Jewish patriot and ardent advocate of freedom of will made homogeneous usage of Stoic perspectives on the idea of people and the world.

- Blaise Pascal

French religious logician and researcher were, at this time, attempting to align the Cartesian ideas of human origins of instinct. His religious idea held both the Stoic and Cathesian emphasis on the autonomy of rationalizing and reasoning, holding that people are on a very basic level reasoning creatures, intrinsically fit for settling on the right choices.

Stoicism has, in general, contend a huge part throughout the ages within the system development of Christian thought further as in Christian ideas, up to date philosophy has taken from Stoicism, a minimum of partially, its conviction that people, in general, should be created as being proximately and primarily connected with the globe.

Contemporary humanism maintains common Stoic principles like the idea in the commonness of people on the premise of common nature and primary reason. It is maybe simply because Stoicism has never become a comprehensive philosophy that, once several centuries of the dissolution of the Stoic College, foundation themes of its philosophy have neem re-emerging and plenty of it became incorporated into trendy philosophy.

Chapter 5

Masters of Stoicism Then and Now

In this chapter, we will take an in-depth look at the various masters of Stoicism with a description of who they are, notable works as well as lessons from each of them. Understanding who these ancient masters are enables anyone to have a deeper connection to Stoicism and the processes that it went through to where Stoicism is in our modern world today.

Seneca

Seneca's philosophy narrowed on the issue of riches and wealth. It seems to be contradicting for a Stoic philosopher to become, at one point, among the richest in Rome. This juxtaposition itself sets him as a unique figure and worth to study. Over 2,000 years ago, Seneca was born in a quiet town in Southern Spain and then moved to Rome to be educated.

In his youth, Seneca focused on politics and have become an upper-level finance clerk. Additionally, he wrote a number of his well-known works like the Consolation to Marcia.

Around 41 A.D with Claudius becoming the emperor, Seneca's life took a drastic turn and he was exiled by the emperor due to allegations of adultery with the emperor's niece.

While his time in exile, Seneca wrote a letter to console his mother while he was in exile. It would be 8 years before Seneca returns to Rome thanks in part to Agrippina, wife of Claudius and mother to future emperor Nero who have asked for Seneca to become Nero's tutor and advisor.

Nero would grow up to become one of the most tyrannical and notorious emperors in the Roman Empire history, which then raised more concerns about Seneca's character. Seneca's wealth was largely in part through his service as Nero's educator. Seneca's death is also in part to Nero's orders who was under the impressions that Seneca was part of a plot to assassinate Nero, replacing him with Gaius Piso. Seneca died in 65 AD. Stoicism still remained constant in Seneca's life, despite all the turbulent episodes in his personal life.

Seneca's introduction to Stoicism is from Attalus, who was also a Stoic philosopher and among Seneca's early teachers. Seneca was also a Cato admirer, but he did not only confine himself to Stoicism. Seneca, in his writings and teachings, borrowed liberally from other schools of thought such as from Epicurus.

Seneca's influence grew after his death with notable figures quoting and learning from his such as Francis Bacon, Erasmus, Montaigne, and Pascal. Strong interest in him also continued in modern-day Stoicism and one of the biggest quotes is from author and trader, Nassim Taleb, who dedicate a whole chapter to Seneca in his book. Tim Ferriss, entrepreneur and writer who published an audiobook also sites Seneca.

He understood well enough that he was not perfect and went through difficult paths in life. Seneca's life is one colored with the ideals of politics to power, ambition to wealth. Despite it all, he is also extremely well known for his introspective understanding and self-awareness of life and subjects of philosophy.

Works & Readings by Seneca

Seneca's writings and work have been declared as among the most enjoyable and readable works compared to other ancient philosophers. This is in part due to most of his work being in the form of letters. If you want to explore more of Seneca's work, here are some recommendations for you:

On the Shortness of Life

This is a trilogy of short letters which offer one of the best introductions of who Seneca is as a philosopher. On the Shortness of Life, he talks about TIME as a non-renewable element in our lives. HIs most famous quotes from this letter are "We are not given a short life, but we make it short, and we are not Ill-supplied but wasteful of it."

Letters from a Stoic

Seneca was one who gave excellent advice to those who seek it from him. These letters make for profound reading and you can also use them as a guide to help you overcome the problems you face in life from grief, despair, depression, success and other issues we deal with. You can read or listen to these writings through audiobooks which you can listen to the collection "The Tao of Seneca" produced by Tim Ferriss.

You can also look at Seneca's plays, Dying Every Day, which offers an excellent biography of Seneca. Look out for Antifragile that contains a dedicated chapter of him by Ferriss. If you are looking for something more scholarly, then the academic paper "Seneca on Trial" offers more in-depth readings.

Lessons and Exercises from Seneca

#1 Find a Role Model

In this correspondence to Lucilius, Seneca urges him to choose the right role model who can provide a good standard of living. This idea is not unique to Stoicism - Stoics do have a role model to emulate. However, Seneca stresses the reason and importance of it. The person we choose to emulate can provide us with the right principles that enable us to navigate through the most difficult and trying of times. It also sets standards for ourselves so we can be the judge of our own behavior.

#2 Never Be a Slave of Your Worldly possessions

Despite the fact that Seneca was known for his wealth as well, he was known to be never dependent on it. According to Nassim Taleb, Seneca was the master of his riches and not its slave. Following this observation, we too need to re-examine our relationship with the material possessions that surround us. Are we trapped by it, being so scared to lose it or can we live freely without it? Seneca concluded his attitude of not being a slave but a master of good fortune "For the wise man regards wealth as a slave, the fool as a master."

#3 Fight Your Ego

Seneca was well aware of how ego can impede our thoughts from progressing and learning. This rings true especially in our day and age where everyone is used to only hearing praise and never criticism. The more praise we get, the more we buy into it, which is how tyrannical leaders are borne. When you keep hearing that you are like God and treated like that, you start to believe it.

Marcus Aurelius

Born nearly two millennia ago, the Roman Emperor Marcus Aurelius was a great leader and a role model, especially on Stoic principles. Born into a prominent family, there was little known of his childhood despite his family being established in Roman society. However, there are greater reports of him as a young man who was into hunting, boxing and wrestling. Hadrian, the reigning emperor at the time of his teenagerhood, was not only old but also heirless, which is why a successor, at the very least, was imperative. Hadrian's first choice, Lucius Ceionius died unexpectedly and so his next choice was Antoninus, a senator at the time who was also childless. As per Hadrian's condition, Antoninus adopted Marcus as well as Ceionius's son, Lucius Verus as his sons and that was how Marcus was known as Marcus Aurelius Antoninus.

Upon Hadrian's death, Marcus was the clear choice as successor as emperor. His education was the focus and he had the privilege to study under Herodes Atticus, who was a rhetorician from Athens as well as Marcus Cornelius Fronto who taught in Latin. The correspondences between Marcus Aurelius and Marcus Cornelius survives to this day.

Marcus would also serve as a consul twice, which meant he would be receiving a valuable and practical education. When Antoninus died in 161, this ended one of the longest reigns in the Roman

Empire. Marcus Aurelius subsequently became the next Emperor and ruled for another two decades until he died in 180. Marcus's reign was not an easy one. He had to deal with the wars from the Parthian Empire, the barbarian tribes from the North, the rise of Christianity and plagues that killed his people.

Before his death, Marcus made his son Commodus his co-emperor. Cassius Dio, the historian at the time describes Marcus's attitude towards Commodus as "amid unusual and extraordinary difficulties he both survived himself and preserved the empire. Just one thing prevented him from being completely happy, namely, that after rearing and educating his son in the best possible way he was vastly disappointed in him."

Marcus held one of the most powerful positions in the ancient world. He knew that nothing would be off limits to him so he could if he wanted to, indulge and succumb to temptations. We have known throughout history that absolute power leads to corruption and yet, Marcus did not fall into these temptations and instead, proved himself worthy of the powerful position that he is in.

Historian Edward Gibbon noted in the book 'Five Good Emperors' that under Marcus's reign, the Roman Empire was governed with both virtue as well as true wisdom. It was this that his subjects saw that put in a class above the rest and a huge distinction from the rest of Rome's past leaders and even those that came after him.

Meditations, among his most famous works, was written in the last few years of his life. It contained his most private and intimate thinking of the world and events around him, especially at a time when he was once the most powerful person on earth. He admonished himself on how to be even more virtuous, just, wise and immune to temptation.

Stoicism provided a solid framework for Marcus in dealing with the pressures and temptations of daily life. Marcus embraced the Stoic studies and thanks to his teacher, Rusticus for introducing him to its teachings as well as the Stoic leader Epictetus. Heraclitus was another strong influence on Marcus as well as to Stoicism. The tragic thing about Marcus was, upon his death, the principles which he led Rome by - duty, self-restraint, respect for others- were abandoned by the imperial line.

Works & Readings by Marcus Aurelius

Marcus was known for two things. One, as the last Good Emperor and two, for personal diary Meditations which was never intended for publication. Meditations are touted as one of the greatest books written in history, but it is also the only book of its kind. The writings explore personal ethics, self-discipline, humility, strength, and self-realization on a definitive engagement. It became the source of inspiration for other writers such as Ambrose Bierce and Robert Louis Stevenson as well as for politicians such as Wen Jiabao, Theodore Roosevelt, and Bill Clinton.

Gregory Hays says that for centuries, traces of Mediations were lost until, in the 10th century, it started appearing in scholarly letters. To explore more, you can also read the Hays's translation and for further reading- The Inner Citadel and Philosophy as a Way of Life penned by Pierre Hadot which focuses on the studies of men behind the work.

You can also get an in-depth insight into works inspired by Marcus, such as The Obstacle is the Way.

Lessons and Exercises from Marcus

#1 Practice to Exercise your Virtues

When we start telling ourselves that we do not possess certain talents, we begin to start self-pity and, in this process, we miss out on the stuff that we possess. We need to stop ourselves from doing this and instead, focus our energy on things that we already possess inside us, which is our capacity and potential for virtuous action.

#2 Reap Strength from those around you

In Meditations, Marcus wrote notes to himself that served as reminders and in times of challenges and difficulty, he would often write words of encouragement, notes to motivate himself and writings of his duty. If we were to learn from Marcus, that would be the element to draw strength from the people in our lives or look at the people that inspire us.

#3 Focus on The Present

Marcus was aware of all the temptations that existed that would make our imaginations run wild, and envision all the ways that these things could go wrong. This exercise is, of course, useful so we can prepare ourselves for the future and make us ready for any kind of adversity. However, Marcus also knew that crippling fear would prevent us from looking forward and thus, paralyze us from getting into action. While it is always ideal to look at the various touch points to prevent disasters from happening, we must also be open to act in the future.

Epictetus

Born 2,000 years ago in Hierapolis as a slave to a wealthy household, Epictetus was given permission by his then owner-Epaphroditus to pursue liberal studies. His pursue on liberal studies was what opened Epictetus to the philosophy of Stoicism and further exposure was through the teachings of someone who would eventually become his teacher and mentor, Musonius Rufus.

Soon after, Epictetus obtained his freedom after when Emperor Nero passed away and he began his philosophical teachings in Rome for 25 years. Unfortunately, Emperor Domitian placed a ban on all philosophers from Rome. Epictetus then fled to nearby Greece, settling in Nicopolis, where he began a school and continued teaching till his death.

It is learned that someone purchased Epictetus' earthenware lamp for 3,000 drachmas. The importance of this lamp can be traced to Epictetus's Stoic principle which states: "I keep an iron lamp by the side of my household gods, and, on hearing a noise at the window, I ran down. I found that the lamp had been stolen. I reflected that the man who stole it was moved by no unreasonable motive. What then? Tomorrow, I say, you will find one of earthenware. Indeed, a man loses only that which he already has."

James Stockdale, a POW for 7 years in Vietnam, credits Epictetus for providing him the blueprint of how to endure tortures he was being subjected to. Stockdale recalled Epictetus' own disabled leg, which he equated his own bound leg as a POW. Stockdale reminded himself of the principle by Epictetus' that physical disabilities are merely an obstacle of the body. It does not need to interfere in our ability to choose unless we make it our choice to choose.

Say this to yourself with regard to everything that happens and you will begin to see that these obstacles are mere hindrances to greater things. In author Tom Wolfe's novel, A Man in Full, Epictetus is featured prominently in it and even psychologist's Albert Ellis's Cognitive Behavioral Therapy was also influenced by Epictetus teachings.

Epictetus never wrote down his teachings, but it was his student Arrian that has taken up upon himself to have a written account of all these teachings. We can find guidance and strength as well as solace in Epictetus' lessons, it is there if we only choose to read and follow it.

Works & Readings by Epictetus

If you are starting with Epictetus, then his Enchiridion, or 'a small handbook' in English is a good place to begin as it is an excellent introduction to Epictetus as it is full with short Stoic maxims and principles.

Epictetus' book though, is difficult to read unlike the works of Seneca and Marcus. The next book or work to consider would be Discourses, which is a longer read and takes a while to comprehend and understand. You can also start on James Stockdale's autobiography Courage Under Fire if you find Epictetus' works too much of a commitment as a start. There is also A Man in Full by Tom Wolfe.

Lessons and Exercises from Marcus

#1 Keep in mind what you can control

The most important principle is to always remember that there are only certain things that you can control while there is a lot that you cannot. You are reminded not to get upset and angry, especially when it concerns someone else's feelings and events that are outside our ability to control. We need to remind ourselves that only our feelings and our behavior are what we need to check and balance. We are always reminded that we need to let certain things go and accept things as they are, which is key to a more fulfilling life. Yet at the same time, a powerful reminder that our actions and choices are fully in our own control.

#2 Set the Standard

Good leaders rarely talk about how things should be done. Instead, they allow their actions to speak for themselves. You need to think about a role model of yours and the lessons that you indirectly received from the choices that they made as well as the examples that they have set in place. In the same essence, we also need to be focused on how we are actually living and the various choices we make because this will ensure that our energy and time is spent well.

#3 Create a Character for Yourself

Human beings are habitual creatures, which is something Epictetus was very well aware of. We often think that there's only one way to do certain things only because it has become a habit for us. In this sense, Epictetus encourages his students to set principles as well as priorities for themselves to follow. Setting this also prevents people from straying too far from it.

Epictetus was aware of how much we human beings act out of habit and how we think that our ways of doing certain things are set in stone. He encouraged his students to set standards and principles that they are required to follow and not stray far away from it. With daily reminders on which way to take and what choices we ought to make, we eventually become closer to the characters we wish to be and have.

Throughout this book, you have heard plenty of times the names of Epictetus, Marcus Aurelius, as well as Seneca. What about modern-day Stoic gurus? Do they exist? Are their teachings in line with Stoicism? Can I use these values in this modern-day setting?

Modern Day Stoic Thinkers

In this chapter, we will look at some of the brightest stars of Stoicism so you can be able to answer if their values, understanding, and principles can really be used in today's world.

If you are new to Stoicism and you are looking for a Guru or a role model to follow and emulate, these modern Stoics can help you understand Stoicism in its modern context. However, understanding the root and foundations of Stoicism is as important as practicing it.

#1 Massimo Pigliucci

Born on 16 January 1964, Pigliucci was a former co-host of the Rationally Speaking Podcast and also the former editor in chief of Scientia Salon, an online magazine. He is an advocate of science education, secularism and a great critique of creationism as well as pseudoscience. He is also a strong advocate for modern Stoicism.

Born in Monrovia, Liberia and raised in Rome, Italy, Pigliucci is a fellow Advancement of Science America and the Committee for Skeptical Inquiry. He also earned a philosophy of science from the University of Tennessee.

During his tenure as the professor of ecology and evolution at the Stony Brook University, Pigliucci researched genotype-environment interactions, phenotypic plasticity as well as natural selection, focusing on the obstacles in natural selection through genetic and development makeup of organisms.

Pigliucci received the Theodosius Dobzhansky Prize in 1997 while working at the University of Tennessee.

Pigliucci, as a philosopher, is focused and continuously interested in the foundations of evolutionary theory, particularly the relationship between philosophy and science as well as the relationships between sciences with religion. Pigliucci pens his thoughts and opinions regularly for the Skeptical Inquirer and Philosophy Now on topics such as intelligent design, climate change denial, and pseudoscience as well as philosophy.

Massimo's Views on Stoicism

Massimo has been practicing Stoicism for about two years and regularly blogs about his opinions, points of view and information on Stoicism at How to Be A Stoic. His piece in the New York Times of the same name became one of the most shared and viewed articles on Stoicism.

Massimo tried studying Buddhism for a while, but he felt that some parts of it were too alien and were wrapped in linguistic, cultural and conceptual terms that he felt, did not relate to him. On the other hand, when Massimo started opening up to the teachings of Marcus, Epictetus or Seneca, he felt more at home and in sync with the teachings and principles.

To Massimo, he feels plenty of people have not been exposed to Stoicism, which is why he continuously pens his thoughts on his blog, recounting his exploration with Stoicism. He states that Stoicism has changed his life for the better, so he hopes that it will also change other people's lives too. He elaborates the ways Stoicism has changed his life. For one, he starts his day with a meditation that is influenced by a Stoic quote, followed by quiet contemplation.

He is also mindful of what happens throughout the day and ends his day retiring in a quiet corner to write his personal philosophical diary. Doing this daily, he feels he is much calmer and can tackle problems with more equanimity than before.

Massimo's foray into Stoicism began when we read a link to Stoic Week on his Twitter feed and thinking nothing much of it, decided to retweet it anyway. The following year was when he really took a closer look to the point where he found himself co-organizing STOICON and even authoring the book 'How to Be a Stoic: Using Ancient Philosophy to Live a Modern Life.

The most important aspect of Stoicism to Massimo is its harmonious connection between practice and theory. He was always trying to live by virtues and ethics, but it wasn't until he took Stoicism seriously did he realize that this philosophy was something that he wanted to keep practicing. To Massimo, Stoicism offers a beautifully constructed, yet sufficiently flexible, mode of thought that can guide one's life day by day.

Massimo believes the Stoicism matters in today's world, the same way it mattered to the Romans and the Greeks- it helps us navigate our lives where large events take place outside of our control and in a place where we continuously seek tranquility and meaning. Human nature hasn't changed much despite the different times that we are living in.

#2 William B Irvine

William grew up in mining towns in Nevada and Montana. As his father was a construction engineer, he stayed in one place long enough till something was built, which was usually 12 to 18 months.

William's education began at a two-room schoolhouse which house 1 to 3 graders and another one for 4 to 6 graders. He obtained a BA in Philosophy and Mathematics at the University of Michigan, followed by an MA and Ph.D. at UCLA in Philosophy. Post Ph.D., it was more of a nomadic career with teaching stints at the Cal State, Los Angeles than at the Pacific Lutheran University followed by the University of Cincinnati. Since 1983, Williams has been teaching at the Wright State University in Ohio.

William's research has always been focused on 'pure philosophy' on topics that were traditionally philosophical. His doctoral thesis was on phenomenalism and he continued with his first publication, "Russell's Construction of Space from Perspectives." He admits that this was the point where he lost his interest in the pure subjects and instead, focused his research on the elements that lie within the border of philosophy and 'something else.'

William's Stoical outlook look on things that other philosophers do not look at. William's practice of Stoicism is extremely close to the ancient Roman Stoics. His believes that despite the world and times changing, human nature is still very much unchanged and with Stoicism, we humans learn how to deal with events and nature.

William's Views on Stoicism

William says that while it may be challenging to practice Stoicism at first, but when we do focus on the practice, it becomes part of our lifestyle. You experience a long stretch of tranquil living. Before he became an ardent believer in Stoicism and eventually a Stoic, William like Massimo, delved into Buddhism. At this time, he wrote the book On Desire: Why We Want What We Want (Oxford University Press, 2005) so he could take a closer look at Buddhism.

During the research of this book, William delved into human desire and among these philosophers, he looked into were the Stoic philosophers such as Seneca and Epictetus. William strives to place importance in both his academic outlook as well as his philosophical outlook for Stoicism. To him, anyone practicing Stoicism must know the ancient philosophy but also adopt these philosophies in life. Not applying Stoic practices will lead to an unhappy existence. He denounces those that study philosophy only to make a good living and not really to attain a good life.

#3 John Sellars

Sellars attended university in 1991 pursuing philosophy. Since that time, he has always been involved with anything related to Stoicism. A large portion of his academic work focuses on peeling the many different aspects of Stoicism and its influence on society. He has written two books on Stoicism, The Art of Living and Stoicism.

John's interest in Stoicism began when he first started studying philosophy and the two main philosophers that he was most attracted to was Nietzsche and Spinoza. Nietzsche, according to Sellars, was someone who acknowledges the connection while at the same time, was very aware of the differences in Stoicism.

At the same time, Sellars was also studying Greek philosophy, which is why he has a great admiration to Socrates as well as Diogenes the Cynic. He also read Epictetus and Marcus Aurelius at the same time to understand each of these person's journey into Stoicism and when they were fully aware of their Stoic status.

Sellars View on Stoicism

One of the most important things in Stoicism that John relates to is called 'reality principle' which both Marcus and Epictetus insisted that humans face up to in finding ourselves and the human condition in general. Sellars advocates that we cannot control each and every element of our lives and when bad things happen, we must just accept it. Like many of the Stoics mentioned here, Sellars also feels that the issues discussed by Seneca or Marcus or Epictetus continue to be relevant to this day. These issues, according to Sella are issues that relate and reflect any person at any point, which is why reading their works can benefit the potential Stoic or those who are looking for a sense of direction.

While he doesn't think everyone should become a Stoic, he does feel that modern society can read their works and open up a possibility of addressing the issues that they are facing. This is also a way of reconnecting with the conventional tradition of thought that has played a vital part in Western culture for so many decades. He points out that plenty of people exposed to Stoicism for the first time are struck by how familiar some of the ideas are, perhaps unaware of the influence Stoicism has had on so many different parts of our shared culture.

Sellars practices Stoicism by having a number of sustained periods, just reading Stoic authors over the past twenty years. He has no doubt that he has been internalizing this all the way and credits Seneca's On the Shortness of Life for helping him fight procrastination on more than one occasion.

Chapter 6

Disciplines of Stoicism

From the very beginning, Stoicism has always placed emphasis on the categories of philosophical discourse and these categories has been divided into three themes, which are 'Ethics,' 'Physics' and 'Logic.' These discourses have roots and foundations into almost every possible Stoicism principle.

Before we go on, a note to say that philosophy itself was unified, to begin with, but theoretical discourse in the Stoic sense would be responsible for categorizing philosophy in this way which is why Stoicism is known for its three major elements.

So far the only Stoic teacher whose work survived in large amounts to this day is Epictetus'. You can find four volumes of Discourses still available for reference and use in our modern-day society. Unfortunately, for the other four volumes, it is lost. Modern Stoics also have a more compressed version of these teachings, which are compiled in Enchiridion. Epictetus lived four centuries after the founder of Stoicism, Zeno. By the time of Epictetus' death, formal Stoic schools have begun ceasing to exist.

Epictetus was the only one who chiefly defined and described the three disciplines of Stoicism and this is something scholars of today cannot find in any other Stoic literature. In this chapter, we will discuss the three disciplines, which are:

- "The Discipline of Desire," relating to the acceptance of faith and fate
- "The Discipline of Action," relating to the love of mankind or philanthropy
- "The Discipline of Assent," concerning mindfulness and how we judge things

Emperor Marcus Aurelius was taught by philosophers who were also heavily influenced and taught by Epictetus. Marcus, Stoicism' best known modern readers unfortunately never got to meet the man. Discourses, recorded by Arrian, was given to Marcus by one of his teachers as part of the study material.

In plenty of ways, Marcus has referred to these teachings which you can definitely see in The Meditations and it also goes to show how Marcus was chiefly influenced by this particular strain of Stoicism.

Marcus uses extensively the Three Disciplines that are elaborated in Discourses, which also provides one of the main elements to interpret his very own writings.

How do we interpret Stoic disciplines?

Pierre Hadot, the French scholar, wrote an in-depth assessment of Meditations in his own book called The Inner Citadel in 1998. In this book, Pierre examines in great details the Three Disciplines while at the same time utilizing it as a framework for his exposition.

If we were to use Hadot's interpretation as a guide, then you would be able to have a clear and comprehensive framework for understanding Stoicism' teachings.

By now, you should already know that the philosophy of Stoic living was to live in accordance with nature or to live harmoniously with it. Hadot states that all three disciplines are created to help all those who are looking to live in harmony and also combining all these three disciplines gives you the secret to a harmonious and serene path of life, with practical philosophy as the new way of living wisely.

#1 The Discipline of Desire

As indicated by Hadot, the train of "desire" is the use of day by day living of the Stoic hypothetical theme of "material science," which incorporates the Stoic investigation in normal logic, religious philosophy, and cosmology.

The discipline concerning desire is the application of living in agreement with the laws of nature. It is a universal concept and in line with the readings and dialects of religious Stoic philosophy, which is with God or with Zeus. In the discipline of Desire, this involves employing a state of mind that is philosophical, which is geared towards the existence and acknowledgment of Fate as an important and unavoidable aspect of life.

This discipline is enticing to see especially as it involves the cardinal ethics related with restraint over the silly interests, which are "strength," or perseverance despite dread and enduring, and "self-discipline" (balance), or the capacity to revoke desire and refuse false or undesirable joys.

'Amor Fati' is what Hadot calls the objective of this discipline or the acknowledgment of one's destiny. This train of thought is summed up in a standout amongst the most striking sections from the Enchiridion: "Look not for occasions to occur as you wish but rather wish occasions to occur as they do and your life will go easily and peacefully."

Cato of Utica, the Stoic hero, was known for his famous march with the surviving Republican armed forces. These armed forces marched valiantly through the hot African deserts together with Cato to make a last-ditch attempt and a brazen call against the tyrannous Julius Caesar, who looked to oust the Republic and announce himself the righteous ruler of Rome.

Despite losing the war, Cato would still become a legend in Rome and even the Stoics declared him "the invincible Cato". Invincible all because of his strong determination when it came to being conquered. Cato rather detached his own intestines with his bare hands than faced the prospect of Ceasar's ruling. He was sure he would be abused and beaten under Caesar's rule; he took it upon himself to die in the most honorable way, which is why he is a legend in Rome.

Marcus Aurelius, centuries later would also lead his weakened army into battle to defend and protect Rome against barbarian hordes. Despite a devastating plague, plenty of misfortunes and invades, Marcus prevailed to victory. Should he had failed, Rome would be no more. As we'll see, the discipline of action clarifies this odd oddity: by what method can the Stoics join acknowledgment with such popular perseverance and gallant activity for the sake of equity?

#2 The Discipline of Action (Stoic Philanthropy)

The discipline of action is the utilization of daily Stoic living according to the theoretical topic of 'Ethics,' which focuses on the life goal of fulfillment or happiness - eudaimonia.

Eudaimonia relates to the Good Life, which all Stoics want to achieve. In the Discipline of Action, it involves the detailing of the Stoic principles concerning virtues of courage, justice, self-discipline as well as wisdom. This discipline is based on the fundamentals of Stoicism doctrine, which relates to the one true good and the one true good that Stoics believe in is virtue. This is sufficient enough for any Stoic to lead a good life and to attain Eudaimonia.

Stoic ethics also cover vices such as irrational and unhealthy passions, craving, fear, emotional pain, and false pleasures. According to Hadot's view, the discipline of action is the basic ideals of living in concordance with the group of all humanity, which implies generously wishing all of humankind to thrive and accomplish "joy" (eudaimonia) the objective of life.

As we also know in Stoicism, another person's wellbeing is not within our control so we must always seek to wish them well, with the Stoic's reverse clause, which seeks to add a caveat of 'Fate permitting' or 'God willing.' As it were, Stoics do their best to act with prudence while tolerating the result of their activities to some degree disengaged way, regardless of whether achievement or disappointment. Additionally, Stoics must act as indicated by their reasonable examination of which outside results are normally to be favored. Subsequently, Marcus Aurelius seems to allude to three clauses that Stoics ought to be consistently careful to connect to the majority of their activities:

- that they are undertaken "with a reserve clause"
- that they are "for the common welfare" of mankind
- that they "accord with value"

#3 The Discipline Stoic Mindfulness

When we talk about Stoic mindfulness, we talk about Assent. Assent concerns the need to apply the daily Stoic ideas of living in accordance with Stoic logic.

Stoicism logic relates to the elements of what we now know as 'psychology' or 'epistemology.' This discipline is the virtue of life in harmony, not just with nature but with rationalization, truthfulness as well as no hidden desires in our actions, mannerism, speech, and thoughts.

It's enticing to see this teaching as specially connected with the cardinal Stoic righteousness of "knowledge" or honesty. According to Hadot, this objective of this discipline is known as the 'inner citadel' as it involves consistent awareness of our true selves as well as the capacity of the mind that is responsible for action and judgment.

Our rational thinking is where our virtue and freedom resides and this is the ultimate in the good in life. As indicated by Hadot's investigation, despite the fact that the Stoics allude to "judgment" when all is said and done (hypolêpsis), they're fundamentally inspired by checking and assessing their own verifiable esteem judgments.

These ideas create the foundations of our desires, emotions, and actions, especially the vices and irrational passions which the Stoics strive to overcome.

Continuously monitoring their judgments enables Stoics to look out for early-warning symptoms that could influence impressions that are unhealthy and upsetting. By seeing this earlier on, Stoics can prevent rather than get carried away by these vices.

The Stoics call this prosochê or "attention" to the ruling capacity of the mind, to our judgments and actions.

Conclusion

As you can most likely observe, these three disciplines cover extensively and are entwined, much the same as the three conventional subjects of Stoic theory, which Hadot claims they're founded on Logic, Ethics, and Physics. In unison, the Stoic has the ability to work towards a more harmonious way of life, which is consistent with nature.

A life in service, according to the Stoics is the natural goal of human natures and the fulfillment of 'eudaimonia' which can only be achieved when you perfect moral excelling and reasoning according to the primary virtues of justice, courage, wisdom, and self-discipline.

Chapter 7

Stoicism in Relationships

To start a conversation about Stoicism and how you can use it in your relationship today, we need to look at Lucius Seneca, an entrepreneur who became a statesman in ancient Rome. Seneca was a philosopher who studied and practiced the disciplines of Stoicism. His life began from humble beginnings and he rose to become one of Rome's wealthiest and most powerful people at that time. Some say he is akin to a modern-day investment banker.

While it is hard to classify what exactly he was back in the day, Seneca can be seen as an entrepreneur who slowly but surely built his fortune, but who also lost most of it and then faced exile for many years before finally returning to Rome. He again started building his fortune. Towards the peak of his wealth, he has become more of a venture capitalist for the Roman state. He tutored the Roman Emperor Nero and was also looked highly upon as one of the wisest Roman men.

Seneca captures the joys of parenting in this writing, clearly demonstrating his love for his family, despite losing his only child. Cato, famously known for Julius Caesar also had great affection for his daughter and Epictetus, another towering Roman Stoic who pushes forth the notion that only lovers of wisdom and rationality can truly understand and appreciate love.

Back to Seneca. His immense popularity and success only turned him into the enemy of the state and towards his death, he faced execution for the crime of being too good. Nero, who eventually became a corrupt emperor would sentence Seneca to die, without thinking and Seneca was, in fact, a master of long-term thinking.

He would strategize to ensure how his teachings would survive and continue growing even after he was gone. He was acutely aware that the state would confiscate and destroy his writings and teachers and he knew he needed to make these antifragile. Seneca compiled his teachings and philosophies into letters which he mailed to specific friends such as Lucilius. These letters would become known as the *Letters from a Stoic*, or sometimes called *Seneca's Epistles*.

Loving Those We Have Properly, While We Still Can

Seneca, in the letter IX of *Seneca's Epistles,* writes and relays his admiration for the story of Stilbo, who was also a practicing Roman Stoic. As a practicing Stoic, he would go through an occasional mental practice of writing things off or even preparing in advance for the possibility of a loss of things. This practice of considering losing what we love and who we love is essentially stoic. It makes us face the present moment with gratitude and it also forces us to engage and ensure that we value those we love today properly while we still have them.

In this letter, Seneca tells a story to illustrate this point with much sympathy and admiration. He begins the story with a stoic named Stilbo who has been traveling far away from home. When Stilbo returned home, he found that barbarians had sacked his city, his entire family killed and his wife dead. Stilbo, in assessing the damaged city was asked 'What have you lost?' to which he answered 'Nihil perditi. Omnia mea mecum sunt!" Or, in English:

"I have lost nothing. My goods are all with me."

At first, you may think that this response and even Seneca's praise of it is extremely cold. However, to understand the deeper meaning of this reaction, we have to look into the Stoic principle on relationships and life. We must acknowledge that the Stoics had an ideal mental state when they pursued life. This state was apatheia.

The State of Apatheia

Apatheia translates more closely to 'Equanimity.' Apatheia is known as the mental state of being undisturbed by lesser emotions. It is a state where nothing can be removed from us because we ourselves have properly valued each and everything, including the people while they were with us.

In the state of apatheia, we do not allow petty annoyances and passions to direct our aims. We accept that we will face losses and that disturbing and distressing events will happen. It is through the recognition that we are prompted to place the right value on our loved ones while they are still around. The Stoics realized that the most consistent and prudent solution to alleviate the stinging bite of future losses was to focus on the ability to rightly value and be content with the relationships that we currently have.

This story that Seneca talks about in his letters to Lucilius is a poignant reminder of this Stoic principle and it also means that the value in Stilbo's story will not be forgotten in history.

Few Thoughts on Apatheia

Apatheia is not an easily attainable element for most of us. As humans, we will definitely find it impossible to value everything and everyone adequately in the present. However, apatheia is still a goal that you need to work towards because of specific reasons and that has to do with lofty goals.

Lofty goals have the tendency to push us towards achieving greater feats and when we fight hard to accomplish what is at first seemingly impossible, we find ourselves actually achieving it or we expand our definition of what is possible. When we are not afraid to cultivate our massive goals, we are elevated to achieve much more than we if had been reasonable with our goals.

Being reasonable or realistic defines your useful purpose. Anyone who has the courage to pursue the state of apatheia is rewarded with more meaning and purpose than what they thought they have gained. In the pursuit of higher goals, we find a higher degree of satisfaction as well as blissful contentment. This pursuit of the unattainable quietly channels us to make better progress, every single day.

Thank You, Next

You may have heard about Ariana Grande (or if you haven't, look her up). She is a singer whose song Thank You, Next, a break-up anthem is about her most recent relationships. Instead of singing about a broken heart, she sings about how each of this relationship has helped her and taught her pain, self-care as well as patience.

This is what apatheia is about when it comes to relationships. This continuous struggle for progress is the only way we can look back on our past and be satisfied with what we have achieved all throughout. The pursuit of apatheia in our present context really means that we create a bank of positive memories which we can always hold on to and reflect to know that we have lived a well-lived life and as we grow older (and wiser), these golden memories make up the memories for our old age.

When it comes to relationships, this pursuit of apatheia is with the purpose of looking back at all our relationships, whether good or bad and realize that it is, in fact, a life full of worthy experiences. No matter what fate brings us, these relationships have been of value and there is good in all of them.

In relationships, apatheia also leads us towards curiosity and growth, helping us to spark better connections and have meaningful conversations.

The Stoic Love

The Stoic love is governed by the idea of a future loss or even a potential betrayal or even the reality that our very own feelings for a person may change over time. To accept these basic conditions makes life a little more manageable when the inevitable does happen. The Stoics, being a lover of virtue, recognizes the virtue in other people.

The Stoic lover will prioritize giving love over receiving it. The Stoic lover can relinquish this love of the specific. Individualized love is important, but it is not the be all and end all for the essence of love. Taking this idea, the Stoic approaches love like a General in the army, equipped with a cool head and a strategic plan. He or she carries out the antidotes of Romantic excess; they are ready to love but will not fall in love. If they do fall in love, as we all humans are inclined to do, they are a way of how to pick themselves up again.

The Practice of Virtues

Stoicism is about two elements:

- The improvement of our character and to become the best version of ourselves
- The realization that much of what happens in this world is outside our control which means we need to constantly recalibrate our expectations about the universe, about life and just about everything else

These principles have a direct influence on the way Stoics view love.

Firstly, with character, the Stoics realize that the best way to improve our character is mindfully practicing the cardinal virtues of Stoicism:

- Practical wisdom- which is the ability to navigate complex situations as best as possible
- Courage- to always do the right thing
- Justice- so we are always aware of what the right is
- Temperance- everything is done in reasonable measure

This practice of four virtues is compatible with various views of love and relationships. We can be monogamous as well as polyamorous, have consensual open relationships or consensual closed relationships, to have sex for the purpose of procreation or specifically for pleasure.

None of these virtues implies that a person lacks practical wisdom, temperance, courage or justice. There are, however, certain things that are always and clearly out of bounds such as cheating on your partner. This is a case of injustice, intemperance as well as cowardice. For a Stoic, this is a definite no-no.

Similarly, if sex is seen as not just a mutually pleasurable activity to share with your partner and only an obsession or a chief pursuit in its own way, then this is seen as being the opposite of being virtuous.

Pleasure and a Loving Relationship

Pleasure, for the Stoic, is another preferred indifferent. It is preferable to pain or in the absence of pleasure as long as it does not get in the way of our virtue. Love is not the same as pleasure.

A loving relationship should always be pleasurable for both parties, but when we talk about pleasure, it is often the physical, the emotional as well as the intellectual. However, if the context of pleasure if given precedence of the love share, then this is a problem which results in the couple or the person losing their ethical bearings.

What about the things that are not in our control? As Epictetus put it, some things are within our control and some are not. What is within our power is opinion, desire, motivation and aversion, basically everything that we do.

That said, whatever that is not within our power does not mean we cannot influence it.

In this context, what does that have to do with love?

We all want to be loved, but according to the Stoics, this thinking is a huge mistake because other people's feelings, their actions as well as their judgments are not within our control.

Instead, we should focus on being the most lovable person for our companion and whether they return this favor or not, it is up to them. We need to do our utmost best. Wanting to control people and the events outside our reach only leads to misery and pain.

For example, the feeling of jealousy is sometimes inevitable in relationships. If we are jealous, it is usually one of two things:

- You do not actually trust your lover
- You are attempting to control something (their behavior) that is outside your sphere of action.

When this happens, you end up becoming miserable and it also will be miserable as well. When you decide to get a grip of your feelings, what you are doing here is being reasonable and project positive emotions and not suppressing your emotions. You are just trying to look at things in a more objective light.

Stoicism teaches us to become better humans by modulating our natural perceptions, desires, and emotions. It teaches us how to become better and act accordingly.

Love Everything that Happens

Another good principle in Stoicism is called the "art of

acquiescence" – to accept rather than fight every little thing.

In most events or scenarios that have taken place especially those that have gone south, we can only change our opinions on them and not the event itself, unless we had a time machine and could go back in time. So, we can only accept what has happened and look forward to these two steps:

- To accept that we don't control everything that happens. We simply must accept it.
- To not only accept, but even love everything that happens. We simply get to enjoy it. It is hard to feel grateful or happy for something that we never wanted to take place, but things happen for a reason and whether it is the desired effect or an unexpected outcome, it happened specifically for you.

You may not understand why it happened, but eventually, you will and you will see how it benefited you.

Our Greatest Asset is our Willpower

Apart from our willpower, we also have other strong assets, which are our decision making and our discipline.

Most of us would not be where we are today if it not had been for our discipline, hard work and our ability to change our circumstances.

We have been accustomed to the fact that by doing right or doing good, the universe will respond in goodness too and it will do what we hope it would do so things will more or less go our way.

Is this true? Do you think this way?

But what if things do not happen the way expect it to? Do we just accept?

Yes. Yes, exactly.

Psychologist Albert Ellis points out our tendency to not accept this but instead of object it. We must move away from the perception and thinking that things must be the way we want them or must be the way we expected.

Stuff will happen to us in life, but it is up to us to choose which ones we want to be okay with and which wants to want to resist. People are going to be a certain way; events will occur as they do. But it isn't just life events.

The solution to all of this is not to fight it with incredible amounts of energy. As Epictetus put it:

Do not seek to have events happen as you want them, but instead, want them to happen and your life will go well.

The Art of Acquiescence

The Stoics referred to the idea above as the art of acquiescence. Abraham Lincoln's favorite quotes pretty much sum it by - And this too shall pass. This is where acceptance is needed.

You may not have to like what is happening to work with current situations, but you can use it to your advantage. However, it starts by looking at the situation clearly and accepting what is happening wholeheartedly. Because that's your only option. The Stoics also used another metaphor called Logos, which is the universal guiding force.

The notion here is that we can struggle with the situation and try our best to challenge it or we can go along for the ride and enjoy it, and along the way learn and make notes in order to change your situation when the tide changes too.

Amor Fati

The thing is, we need to go through setbacks in various forms in order to do great things. Remember that it is pressure that creates a diamond and agitation in an oyster that creates a pearl. We need to love the things we do and sometimes accept what happens as a result, whether it is good or bad. We have to learn to find joy in every single thing that happens.

Once we discard our expectations and accept what happens, there is the moment of understanding that some things (especially bad things) are beyond our control. At this point, we need to love whatever that has happened to us and face forward ahead in life with unfailing cheerfulness. Indifference and acceptance are definitely better than rage and disappointment. Very few people practice this, but it is only the first step.

We do not get to choose what happens to us, but we can always choose how we feel about it. You want to feel good- even if this good feeling does not happen immediately after a bad situation, we will still strive to move towards feeling good and feeling happy. If the event must occur, Amor fati (a love of fate) is the response. Do not waste to ponder even for a second looking at your expectations that did not happen. Face forward, and face it with a smug little grin.

Chapter 8

Stoicism in Business

When it comes to business, nobody wants to fail. We all want to avoid doing as many mistakes as possible, especially rookie ones to ensure that our losses are little to none. Unfortunately, the best way to learn is to fail. Failure is after all our friend in disguise.

That said, understanding all there is to know about the business you are in and equipping yourself with the right know-how, knowledge, expertise, and trends will help you avoid glaring pitfalls.

As the 21st century goes on, business trends move towards a swirling interest around resilience, mindfulness, and innovation to overcome pitfalls and mistakes. Many have trodden this path, leaving us with many lessons for us to learn.

Among these lessons is the brand of ancient western philosophy that is Stoicism. Stoicism focuses on mindfulness as well as resilience. It focuses on the mindset that enables us to flourish and live the Good Life as well as achieving Eudemonia. These guiding principles have had a significant impact on Western ideology and thought process.

Stoicism in business helps us to overcome destructive emotions. Here we again focus on the three most famous Stoics of ancient Rome and derive lessons we can use and practice in business.

- Marcus Aurelius- focused on compassion, humility, and restraint in life
- Epictetus- overcame the horrors of slavery, going on to find his own school of thought
- Seneca- though faced with death from Emperor Nero, was focused on ensuring the comforts of his wife and friends.

At the very core of their teachings are three basic lessons:

- The world is volatile and predictable and life is brief
- We need to be steadfast, strong and in control of ourselves
- Dissatisfaction arises from our own impulsive actions rather than a logic course

If you are looking for a prime example of Stoicism in business as well as in leadership, look no further than the previous Commander-in-Chief, former President Barack Obama who is very obvious in demonstrating stoic qualities through his calm and collected demeanor. Many say that his behavior patterns echo that of Roman stoic, Cato the Younger.

To be stoical is to transform negative emotions into a perspective that prepares you to be in the right state of mind because as well know, our mind, our actions, our reactions are the only things within our control and we ditch the other things that we have no grasp on.

Stoicism in Business

To be stoical in business is to be aware, in control as well as be mindful of what we do, who we engage with, the trends in our industry, expenditure and the day-to-day running of our business entities. We train our minds to be this way rather than get lost in the various emotions and random thought processes that lead us to lose focus on our business goals.

The Stoic exercise, such as practicing misfortune and poverty, really helps business owners to prepare for worst case scenarios rather than just going into a fall sense of success that everything is alright.

When this happens, when we fall into a dull lull, we make no preparations in case the stock market crashes, we do not work on making enough savings, we do not diversify our business plans and most importantly, we do not innovate.

Practicing stoic principles into our business and entrepreneurship as well as in our leadership can help us build resilience and change our state of mind to rebound from knockbacks.

Another Stoic principle is to turn problems into opportunity. If you want to cultivate a culture of creativity in your business, then you need to think of 'The Glass half Full, instead of half empty' and to turn obstacles upside down. Look for an opportunity in every bad situation.

Stoics Lessons for Business, for Leadership

1) Rationality, perspective, and logic

We need to control ourselves first before we reach out control the events that are happening around us. Self-control is the only thing that will bring success each and every time.

2) Authenticity

While having roles models to look up to is healthy, however, emulation can turn into imitation and all you will ever produce is a second-rate product with no ounce of innovation. Stoicism here helps us in embracing our unique quirks and using it to leverage into our business.

3) Self-mastery and purposeful action

A Stoic will know exactly what they want from the get-go. They have clear goals with clear routes to get there. You can channel this by writing your daily goals because when you do this, you create a psychological pre-commitment on what you need to do the minute you wake up and you also create a self-expectation that increases the likelihood of achieving these tasks.

Science continues to prove what the Stoics have known for all these centuries. According to Shawn Achor, a psychologist at Harvard, professionals who worked on gratitude practice each start of their day performed at a much efficient and productive level than those who did not. They also achieved a higher dopamine release that boosted their overall performance, happiness, and mood.

4) Military leaders follow their principles

In 1965, when James Stockdale's plane was shot down over Vietnam, he told himself, 'At least I'm leaving the world of tech and entering the world of Epictetus.' Not something you would have thought of in the event you found yourself in this scenario. Stockdale would spend over 7 years in a Vietnamese prison and during this time, he wrote about Stoicism and how it saved his life. He is quoted as saying "You must never confuse faith that you will prevail in the end—which you can never afford to lose—with the discipline to confront the most brutal facts of your current reality, whatever they might be."

5) Stoicism is ideal for the entrepreneur

As an entrepreneur, having to practice misfortune makes you a stronger person with a stronger mindset, which helps you overcome adversity. You are better able to flip obstacles upside down, turning problems into opportunity and also keeping a perspective of how small you are; you also keep your ego manageable.

6) Stoicism lends itself to globalization

Epictetus shared the poignant reminder- that each of us is a citizen in our own land, but we are also members of the great city of gods and men'. Marcus Aurelius consistently reminded himself to love the world.

As we all rush to meet the changes of this world and continue creating innovations to make this world a better place to live in, we can look towards Stoicism to give us a system that we can cultivate and take relief from what the Stoics call ' a personal operating system for a high-pressured environment.'

We hope this chapter has given you an understanding and a powerful antidote to help you maneuver your way through life and in business

As Marcus Aurelius remarked:

"The things you think about determine the quality of your mind."

Chapter 9

Stoicism in School

If we understand Epictetus's teaching correctly, a sign of the educated is based on the knowledge of the difference between what is within one's control and what is not.

In this chapter, we focus solely on educators. It would be extremely helpful for educators to learn this difference in their professional careers because it will help them to create more fruitful relationships with their students, produce more effective teaching, lessen the burden and mental stress they face as well as prevent any psychological burnout. If we look at Epictetus to help us navigate Stoicism in the educational sphere, then it would help educators become more rational pessimists and expect more will go wrong than right.

Staying Stoical in School

Some of the most profound questions asked when it comes to education and life is:

- What is the best way to live?
- How can we deal with the difficult situations that we face?
- What would it take to improve our minds?

If you have questions like these, then the answers to this lie at the very base of Stoic philosophy. Educators in schools, colleges, and institutions can use their insights on adversity, on the mind as well as on practice to help our students shape the way they think and cultivate a positive thought pattern.

Some two thousand years ago, a teacher, a playwright, and an emperor asked:

Stoicism in school

In school, children learn how to deal with difficult emotions such as worry, frustration, cravings, fear, arguments, temper, gossip, squabbles, jealousy, bitterness, hurt and many other complex emotions. Through stoicism, we can offer more fortifying ways to think about dealing with these difficulties:

Teachers can …

- Show students the things that are always within their control, which are their responses to situations, their thoughts as well as their reactions.
- Show and teach pupils how to anticipate as well as cope with adversity
- Guide students on how they can change their perceptions so that they resent less, complain less. It will also help them to instill and keep a positive perspective, stay grateful, and be happy.

Pupils can learn how to…

- Let go of frustration by realizing that their minds are within their control and they can let go of the irritation that is counterproductive to their goals. This should be released and not dwelt on.

- Let go of unnecessary worries by remembering that the more they worry about things that are outside their control, the worse they will feel. On the other hand, the less they worry, the happier and calmer they are.
- Cope with arguments by avoiding incessant complaining, avoiding criticizing as well as blaming or resenting the people around them. Instead, they can focus on endeavors and feelings of gratefulness and cheerfulness.

School leaders can convey the lives of the thinkers, and their thinking ...

By looking at the leaders of Roman Stoicism, senior leadership teams and leaders can set the foundation of a cohesive and fruitful mind that focuses on things, elements and experiences that are controlled by our own selves.

Epictetus, Marcus Aurelius, and Lucius Seneca were all thinkers who used mantras, analogies as well as writing in diaries, letters, and notebooks. All three were leaders who were also tutors and advisors.

Their main analogies:

Slavery: The irritation that enslaves us whereas wisdom frees us

Illusions: The anxieties that are the products of our own creation and which is something we can get rid of Boxing: To continuously train hard, so we do not let these anxieties bring us down.

Introducing Stoicism to your Students

On their first week of school, you can teach them the approach to life and that everyone experiences difficulties, but we all have it in us to overcome these difficulties. You can do this in assemblies or an hour of lesson. You can also discuss this over group. With stoicism, you teach your students to anticipate the frustrations of life as well as the mantra 'Stay Stoical.'

Here are 6 ways you can use Stoicism in exams, during detention, in arguments, in pain, in sports and also in communicating with your student's families:

- In detention … stay stoical!

Oftentimes, students will feel upset or even resent your giving them detention. In your conversations with them, remind them to stay stoical, calm as well as help them build and keep a perspective of their detention. Teach them to let go of anger, work out the elements that they can control as well as think about how they can build trust in the future. You can also allow them to decide what they want to do differently next time.

- Before, in and after exams … stay stoical!

Of course, tests can be extremely stressful for both children, their parents, as well as the teachers, creating and marking these tests. For students, educators can help them see that preparing, revising and overcoming their procrastination is something that is within their control. If they do fail an exam or perform poorly, remember to tell them to remain stoical and not to allow this minor complication agitate them. Instead, tell them to focus on what they can do differently the next time around and help them with their upcoming assessments.

- In arguments … stay stoical!

When a student gets into an argument with their fellow students or friends, using stoicism here can help to remind both parties to practice calm, ignore vicious rumors as well as ignore gossip and insults. It also helps them to stay positive or rational rather than give in to these negative thoughts and exacerbate anger and mistrust.

- When ill or struggling… stay stoical!

It is definitely a struggle to wake up early and get to school and it is even harder if students are feeling ill. Of course, if they are feeling well but lack the motivation to get up and come to school, use stoicism to help them see that waking up anyway, showing up anyway is something to be proud of. Help students see that some setbacks can be controlled. If they fall, get back up and try again. If they colored outside the lines, then create your own masterpiece. The idea here is that a stoic mindset reduces our fragility. The volatility of the world itself cannot destabilize us. With the use of stoicism, problems can become opportunities as long as we train our resilience.

- At sport … stay stoical!

Sports are competitive by nature and at times, tempers can run high. The use of stoicism here can help students not to over-celebrate their wins and jeer those who did not win a match or score a goal. On the other hand, not winning also teaches us not to despair or put on the blame game. Using stoicism prevents a footballer from turning a yellow card into a red card or from getting a contestant from being disqualified. If there are any setbacks, great- here's a chance to train our willpower.

- With your families … stay stoical!

Growing up, children also face difficult times. As much as we would like to shelter them from the adversities of life, children also face issues and problems of their own with their friends, peers, siblings, and cousins. If they are taught to remain stoical in school, then they can cascade these learnings to their own family life by enabling them to deal with arguments and adversity in their families such as death or divorce. It gives them a good perspective and enables them to remain grateful and not take the people around them for granted. Rather, they develop meaningful relationships with their immediate family members, which then transcends into their adult lives.

Teaching children to remain stoic during tough times creates a powerful perspective for them that helps them to improve their resilience, their relationships and also their lives.

Chapter 10

Seeing the Glass Half Full

In stoicism, you see the world as it is an attempt to not try and change a person's view of things. Simultaneously, stoics also try to work on their minds to act in a way that they will be proud of.

Before we go into the Stoic's idea of the glass half full, here are the various ways in which other philosophies and religion see the glass half full, just to give you an idea:

- Buddhism: The glass doesn't really exist, for nothing does.
- Solipsism: I am the glass. And the whole world is nothing but my alcoholic delirium.
- Islam: There is no glass except glass.
- Judaism: Why only my glass is half empty?
- Orthodoxy: The glass is half empty as a punishment for our sins.
- Catholicism: The glass is half empty only for bad people.
- Freudianism: You were underserved as a child.
- Stoicism: Yes. My glass is half-empty, and I deserve it to be so.
- Communism: Everyone is entitled to a full glass.
- Socialism: Yes, the glass is only half full. But it is equally so for everyone.
- Yoga: You are both the glass and its contents. You and your glass are One.

- Science: The glass contains 1/2 of liquid and 1/2 of air, thus the glass is always full.

When we talk about how an optimist views a glass of water, we usually normally their thought process but saying they look at the glass as being half full.

For a Stoic, the level of optimism is only the starting point. The stoic, after expressing their appreciation that the glass is half full will then go on to express their delight in having a glass. Because, that glass could have been chipped, broken or stolen.

And if they are really bringing their Stoic philosophy in, the Stoic might even go so far as to say that glass vessels are a unique thing. Not only are they cheap but also durable and above all, allows us to see the contents inside. The stoic representation of the glass sounds a bit extensive or silly but take note of how they have given their perspective on it. The stoic shares their capacity of joy and in doing so, have shown you that the world is indeed, a wonderful place.

To a stoic, the glass is amazing, but to everyone else around them, the glass is just another glass and it is a glass that is half empty.

According to William B. Irvine, author of the Book 'A Guide to the Good Life: The Ancient Art of Stoic Joy', the first order of business to understand Stoicism is to realize that in English, stoic means emotionless but it is such a huge difference to the Greek understanding and practice. Stoic, in the Greek sense, is to have elements of tranquility. One can say that it is similar to Buddhism, albeit without Buddhism's insistence of detaching the positive and joyous elements.

So how can the average person practice this aspect of Stoicism- of looking at the glass not only as half full but also as a wonderful thing?

Here are six ways you to see the glass as half full:

#1 Stop comparing yourself to others.

The world is not always about you. In fact, it never was about you. When a neighbor gets a new car or a friend gets a raise or your colleague loses weight and none of this reflects back on yourself, don't fret! Just because you did not get any of those, does not mean you never will. You still have time to improve yourself. All of us hit different milestones in life at different periods of time. Some people get married earlier while some get married later in life, some people end up buying a house before their 30s while you only bought yours at the age of 40. You graduate on time while some friends did not. When we compare ourselves to the people around us, we usually feel worthless and end up not performing to the best of our abilities because we think we've run out of time.

You only run out of time when you are on your deathbed.

#2 Change your focus.

Pessimism and optimism are just nothing more than average feelings we all go through. If you are moping about and wondering why your life sucks, you are bound to be feeling more pessimistic about things. However, use the Stoic approach to shift your perspective and look at the glass full or even the fact that there is a glass and there are contents in it. When you shift your thoughts to something that involves more gratitude, you will feel much more optimistic about the situation you are in and you might also find ways and ideas to better yourself.

#3 Look for positive signs everywhere.

Again, it's all about perception. Look for the good in things and you'll see that you can smile a little bit more. See something that triggers a happy memory? Be grateful. Found a penny on the floor? Pick it up and be grateful. It takes very little to be happy but an enormous energy to be sad.

#4 Listen to uplifting music.

If you find yourself having a bad day or for some reason just feeling pessimistic and down, listen to feel good music. 'Happy' by Pharrell Williams is music so uplifting it is hard not to tap your feet to the sound of the beat. Josh Groban's 'You Raise Me Up' is another motivational music that can help literally, lift you up. Music does have the power to heal so if you ever feel that you are in a pessimistic frame of mind, put some good music on and shake to the rhythm as this will help shift your negative feelings to a positive one.

#5 Detach from outcomes.

The root of optimism lies in knowing that when one opportunity passes, another one will come. As much as we think that that was our window or moment, sometimes there is a reason why we let it go. It may seem to others around you that it was the perfect opportunity for you to act or be in or sign up or explore, but maybe you weren't ready that is why you did not act upon it?

Take a look at your life before this and identify the times where you wanted something but did not get it but looking back, you are glad that things turned out the way it did for you.

#6 Stop saying you are a pessimist.

Words, like music, are a powerful thing. When you start thinking of yourself as good or kind or optimistic, you radiate a good vibe about yourself. People around you feel it and eventually- this becomes who you are. Mention your name and people say you're great to be around with or you're the life of the party or that you are such a positive force to the team. What you feel and think and say will become part of who you are.

Conclusion

This goes to say that always being happy or seeing the glass half full is always good, being optimistic all day, every day may distract you from negative things that are happening around you and prevent you from acting appropriately. Case in point, if someone has lost a family member, you react by giving your condolences and not to say tomorrow is a better day. We need balance at the end of the day and this chapter serves to look at ways to believe in yourself and be optimistic.

Chapter 11

Techniques for Using
Stoicism in Daily Life

If you are really interested in leading a life based on Stoic principles, then here are some exercises that you can do to develop Stoic practices and outlooks. These exercises can benefit the potential Stoic but also be extremely helpful to anyone doing these exercises.

Just keep in mind that Stoicism is a philosophy of life and not something that enables you to achieve spiritual enlightenment. Therefore, these exercises can be used by anyone in this life. They are practical and they also do not need any kind of special tools or equipment, except determination and a functioning brain.

#1 Early Morning Reflection

Early morning reflection has been known to have plenty of benefits and it is greater than just being about planning what you want to do on that day. It is also about your reaction to these things and how others will react as well. You anticipate the things that would take place.

One of the first few things to do in your reflection is be grateful that you have woken up- not many people have this privilege today. Once done, you can then plan out how to embrace your virtues and how to avoid your vices. It doesn't have to be a detailed plan, but it is just something for you to go over.

For instance, it can be a personal strength you want to cultivate-you can think about how you will be incorporating it into your day. Do you want to procrastinate less? Do you want to avoid being part of office gossip? Do you want to arrive at meetings on time? Mentally check how you will be dealing with the difficult situations that will arrive.

Next, you want to remind yourself that only you are in control of your thoughts as well as your actions. Everything else is not your control. You can do your early morning reflection with a walk to enjoy the rising sun or you can even perform some light stretches on your bed and meditate thereafter. Some light exercises using your bodyweight also helps.

#2 A View from Above

The second exercise to practice is designed to remind where you are in this world and the importance you bring. We are not talking about how big a role you play in the scheme of things but really, how small you really are in the course of life. How many lives can you touch being where you are now? How many people are you significant to? This is not about bringing you down and saying that your life is not as important as you thought it was, but it is about relating to the whole world and beyond.

Again, you need to meditate somewhere quit so pick a place such a park on a beach if you live near one. Otherwise, a park will do. Look above starting with the clouds and then slowly bring yourself closer to the world and people. Observe things around you from discoveries, creation, first kisses, traffic jam, the sound of the blaring horn. Observe but do not judge because now, you need to think about how you are related to all of this. How do you see yourself in these situations and know that all these things are only relatively important and that is how you are relatively important?

You are only important to a certain extent. Life existed before you and will continue to exist after you so worry yourself about things that directly involve your being.

#3 Contemplation of the Ideal Person

In this exercise, we will look at a catalyst for change towards becoming your ideal self. Becoming your ideal self is a never-ending quest. The older we get, the more things we know, the wiser we become and we find that our priorities also change. Your ideal persona will continue to change based on your experiences and lessons in life.

But for now, at this moment that you are in, what kind of person do you make yourself to be? What qualities, to you, make an ideal person?

This is not a question that has a straightforward answer. In some respects, it would be easier to ask what an ideal person would do in a situation rather than their characteristics. From the actions of this person, you can then derive their qualities and characteristics and hopefully, emulate them on your own.

You can start by creating a list of your role models, past, present ones that you had the opportunity to get to know, to work with and so on. Determine what their best qualities are and whether you want to emulate this. After all, imitation is the best form of flattery.

You can also make a list of people you do not like and what you do not like about them and then strive to avoid these characteristics.

#4 Cultivating Philanthropy

What is philanthropy? Philanthropy can be defined as a desire to promote and ensure the welfare of other people. We hear about how billionaires and celebrities are philanthropists and the kinds of things they do.

This word is often associated with rich people, people with money. But philanthropy does not only constitute money. In actual fact, having the right attitude and the desire to help people is what makes a philanthropist — not the amount of money.

When we endeavor to do philanthropy, our goals need to be community-centric. It needs to be thinking about the wider scope of our work and how it can bring everyone closer, towards a common goal and a connected circle.

Your family is an extension of yourself and by another extension-the community you live in. These connections go far and wide as the entire country. Hierocles, the Stoic philosopher said we should look at our siblings as an extension of our own.

How does this benefit you; you might ask?

Thinking of yourself as part of a connectivity to your family and community, you end up not becoming overly attached to any single individual. You are your own person, albeit connected in some way or another. This also means you are part of a larger circle of friends, which means you are exposed to a greater set of cultures and viewpoints, giving you an incredible opportunity for learning.

So how do you extend your circle?

You can start by striking up a conversation with someone at your workplace that you barely talk to. You can say YES to a party invitation which you otherwise would have said no to because you prefer being at home. Another thing to do is to ensure that your close friends are aware that you consider them a part of your family and that you can be relied on to be there for them should they need you.

#5: Self Retreat

Self-retreat, whenever possible, is a must. Self-retreat enables you to find peace or freedom, even for a tiny bit, from the regularities of life.

Peace and freedom are the things that come from inside you, so if you are trying to run away from cognitive dissonance, then you are actually running away from yourself. Plenty of people feel that they need to 'go somewhere' or travel in order to find peace of mind.

You can if you want to, but for a cheaper alternative, peace can be found just about anywhere and it all begins with a visit into your mind. Don't get weird out. Nowhere else is anyone as free as in their own mind. You can be anything you want inside your head; you can be as different as you want in your mind. While traveling is wonderful, it's not the only way to find yourself. All you need is to shut yourself out from the world, about five to 10 minutes

According to Marcus Aurelius, people seek retreats to countrysides and seashores or hills for themselves and this has become a habit

You can escape your physical or mental confinement by journeying inside your mind. Those that feel trapped by work or the responsibilities of life feel lifeless and turn into pessimists. Those that are trapped inside mental confinements move towards being depressed or worse.

One of the very best ways to journey without ever having to leave the comforts of your own home is by reading and of course, meditating.

#6 Philosophical Journal

Have you thought of keeping a journal? It could be an online journal or a private blog or you can go old school and actually keep a paperback journal but whatever it is, have you thought about it?

The difference with this journal is that instead of writing about your life and what has happened in it, you instead write about life from a Stoical perspective, meaning you analyze life as a way to discover your shortcomings and track the way you make changes to live according to the Good Life.

After all, constant reflection is what can improve our current circumstances as well as our outlook on the future.

By planning our actions according to an ethical framework, you can then look back and see what you can change based on the scenarios and events that took place. Did you get irritated when you did not get your answer immediately while researching something? Did you snap at the customer service representative for asking too many verification questions? Were you confused after a long meeting with your colleagues about a new project?

Analyzing your day in your Stoic journal can help you work towards changing yourself for the better. A Stoic journal can just your normal journal with an added philosophical entry.

If you want to start a Stoic journal, then best to keep going at it for 21 days (21 days is scientifically proven to cultivate and keep a habit). You can also read the philosophical journal entry by the Roman Emperor, Marcus Aurelius called 'Meditations.'

#7: Understanding That Life Has Layers

In any event or scenario, there are many different layers. Just like an onion, we can do an exercise of stripping away each layer to find out what it represents and what each individual contributes to the scenario.

What is the value that this situation holds for everyone? In most cases, there is no value.

What is the kind of skills that this event or scenario would need? It is great if you have the skills needed, but one good way self-development is viewing the situation without interfering.

For example, let us take a look at a common rite of passage for everyone- growing up and figuring out where we fit in the scheme of things.

As we grow up, we often struggle to find or decide what we want to do in life. Some people have it easy and know immediately what they like and what their passions are and then there are the rest of us who are still trying to find something fulfilling and meaningful to work towards.

Some of us have an excellent start in life while some of us end up doing something for the sake of money and some of us do it because it is expected of us or it's the only way we know.

You know the drill. Go to school, do well, get good grades, graduate, look for a job, find a spouse, get married, have kids and then work and work and work till we die?

Some of us fit into that mold while some of us do not.

So ask yourself this- What would you do if money was not an issue? Answer this question, then work your way towards that. It doesn't mean that you need to quit your 9-5 job straight away, but the idea here is to work towards reaching that goal, incrementally.

#8 Bedtime Reflection

We started this series of exercises with a morning reflection and we end the day with a night reflection. Your reflection should focus on what has taken place in your day today and not about what is going to happen.

Mentally go through the things that happened in your day and ask yourself if:

- Did you behave according to your principles?
- You treated the people with whom you interacted with in a friendly and considerate manner?
- What vices did you fight?
- Did you make yourself a better person by cultivating your virtues?

In your Stoic journal, you can also write down your reflections and you can also plan the next day too. Write down your notes and what you want to reflect on in the morning. What you do today will link up with tomorrow morning's reflection.

In your journal, write down what you want to improve the next day. It doesn't have to be a big thing. Write it down, no matter how small the improvement may be. If you keep this up for 21 days, you'd be surprised how much you can and would be able to change.

Along with your notes, also remind yourself that this day has ended and there is no way you can change anything about it unless you time traveled. What has happened, has happened. The sun will rise tomorrow.

#9 Negative Visualization

Negative visualization is an exercise focused on giving us a reminder of how privileged we are, even when we think we are not. It is a simple idea, but one that has an enormous impact. All any of us need to do is to imagine that terrible things have taken place or, good things have not taken place. Keep in mind that this is not an exercise steering you into negativity. It is simply giving you an idea of the scale of catastrophe:

You lost your wallet. But it could be worse - you could have lost all your possessions

You are set up on a blind date. But it could be worse- you could have married without ever meeting your spouse beforehand.

Your aunt met in an accident and is in the hospital recovering. It could be worse- she could have died.

You met with an accident and fractured your arm. It could be worse- you may have been paralyzed.

You can also imagine how situations that you are about to embark on will go wrong.

This kind of therapy is not cultivating pessimism, but instead, it makes you realize that things could get worse and things could turn bad, but it has not and it did not happen to you.

In doing this exercise, you can try and imagine some catastrophes that could take place in the act that you are about to do or the situation that you are in. Maybe you could imagine having born in a time that you would miss having the convenience of the internet or being born at a time when women were not allowed to vote? Or traveling to far off places could only be done through sailing.

#10 Physical Self-Control Training

In this exercise, we look at physical hardships and going without the stuff we enjoy. This exercise, if you look at it, is a practical version of the exercise above.

In this exercise, it serves to achieve two purposes:

- To prepare ourselves to have hardships
- To be happy with what we have and not to desire the things that are not within our control.

Everything in life should be grasped loosely, like sand through our hands. You do not hold sand tightly because if you do, it escapes your grasp.

These are a few examples that you can try in your physical self-control:

- Eating only one meal a day
- Drinking water only for a certain period of time
- Not having baths instead only timed showers
- Only having the option of one phone call a day

The point of doing all of the above and anything else that you can think of is that you need to view everything as a transient from yourself to the things you own to everyone you know- all of this will cease to exist.

The best way forward is to view everything on a loan so instead of having to say "I have lost it," you switch your perception to "I have given it back." Reflect on your situations and realize that you did not lose anything but merely, returned it back. In doing so, you also create an optimistic view.

To get started on this, you can change something in your daily routine to make your day a little harder. Maybe instead of driving to work, take the bus. Maybe instead of having your chia seed pudding, skip your breakfast and only have coffee. Maybe go without the internet for a day?

Bottom line

The exercises stated in this chapter helps you cultivate Stoic thinking in a modern-day setting. You can always do two or three exercises together, such as taking a morning walk and reflecting at the same time but choosing now to wear a jacket and being grateful for the crisp morning air. You've successfully done self-control and negative visualization while going on your morning walk and reflection. Stoicism is not hard and complicated. You need to understand its values before you dismiss it. Also, you do not need to call yourself a Stoic in order to practice Stoicism.

The main denominator behind all of these exercises is that they only require you to take a long and hard look at yourself and the way you live your life. This is never a bad thing, no matter what viewpoint you look at life.

Conclusion

We hope you now have a better and clearer understanding of Stoicism, its disciplines, as well as its principles and how you can apply them in your daily life. You can look at this book as a means of self-realization and self-help because it does facilitate cognitive, behavioral as well as emotional improvement in your life.

Focusing on what we can control and letting go of what we cannot, to us seems to be a pretty positive way to lead our lives. Often, we let the little things get to us and with this Stoic principle in mind, it helps us stay focused on what really matters.

Even practicing misfortune, in asking ourselves- what could go wrong, can not only prepare us for whatever tests that may come our way, but it also helps us troubleshoot problems in our work, in life and relationships.

As mentioned at the start of this book, the Stoic philosophy offers a broader philosophical perspective so even if you do not intend to lead a life based on the Stoic philosophy, you can still practice some of its principles to make your life better.

While Stoicism has withered away for some time, it is now coming back in its full glory, with new-age philosophers bringing in Stoicism to fit the modern world. You may not agree with all aspects of Stoicism, but the idea here is to use some of its principles to work on the areas of life that you feel need repair or need help in.

Hopefully, this book will further inspire you to read more about what the ancient philosophers have written down, such as books and writings from Seneca, Epictetus, Marcus Aurelius.

If you enjoyed this book, please let me know your opinion by leaving a short review on Amazon. Thanks!

Made in the USA
Middletown, DE
03 September 2019